Israel in Crisis

Also By David Dolan

Israel in Crisis

What Lies Ahead?

David Dolan

Fleming H. Revell
A Division of Baker Book House Co
Grand Rapids, Michigan 49516

© 2001 by David Dolan

Published by Fleming H. Revell
a division of Baker Book House Company
P.O. Box 6287, Grand Rapids, MI 49516-6287

Fifth printing, July 2003

Previously published in 2001 by Oracle House

Printed in the United States of America

ISBN 0-8007-5804-8

Library of Congress Cataloging-in-Publication Data is on file at the Library of Congress, Washington, D.C.

Unless otherwise indicated, Scripture quotations are from the NEW AMERICAN STANDARD BIBLE ®. Copyright © The Lockman Foundation 1960, 1962, 1963, 1968, 1971, 1972, 1973, 1975, 1977, 1995. Used by permission.

Scripture quotations identified KJV are from the King James Version of the Bible.

For current information about all releases from Baker Book House, visit our web site:

http://www.bakerbooks.com

The LORD is good,
A stronghold in the day of trouble,
And He knows those who take refuge in Him.

Nahum 1:7

Contents

═

THE MIDDLE EAST

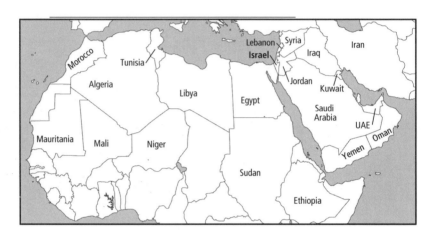

Then it will happen on that day that the Lord
Will again recover the second time with His hand
The remnant of His people, who will remain
From Assyria, Egypt, Pathros, Cush, Elam, Shinar,
    Hamath,
And from the islands of the sea.

Isaiah 11:11

Introduction

===

The telephone rang in my southeast Jerusalem apartment. It was Richard Frieden, a close friend who used to serve on the Jerusalem police antidrug squad and now heads a powerful youth ministry. I could tell right away that he was calling from his car cell phone. "Do you know what in the world is going on?" he asked excitedly after informing me that he was stuck in stalled traffic near the historic Old City. As a journalist who has lived and worked in Israel since 1980, I often get calls from friends asking me for the latest scoop. "Well, it sounds pretty serious," I replied, reacting to the cacophony of sirens wailing in the background. "I suppose some Muslims are rioting on the Temple Mount," I opined, adding that if that was the case, it was "just like in the days when I was reporting from there every Friday during the Palestinian uprising."

I quickly phoned a journalist colleague and determined that my assessment was correct. He told me that hundreds of Palestinians had just come out of the Friday prayer service on the disputed holy site and were clashing with Israeli security forces. He said some Arabs had already been killed in the fighting, and others had been wounded. Soon I went to work reporting on what quickly became known as the "Al-Aksa uprising," a major story that rapidly captured the attention of people throughout the Middle East and the entire world.

My first book, *Holy War for the Promised Land* (which has been updated several times, most recently under the title *Israel at the Crossroads*), was published in 1991. It begins with a report on a violent clash on the Temple Mount that left seventeen Palestinians dead—the worst one-day death toll in the original uprising that lasted from late 1987 until 1993. It is no coincidence that the book you are now reading, coming out exactly one decade later, is beginning in much the same way. As the Bible says, there is really nothing new under the sun.

This time, however, it is not just Palestinians and Israelis who are in a state of violent crisis. The entire Middle East seems poised on a knife-edge. The sense that the region was heading toward another full-scale war sharply increased after Islamic terrorists destroyed the famous twin towers of New York's World Trade Center and a portion of the Pentagon in September 2001.

The original uprising, as traumatic as it was, did not have the same ominous dimensions as the one that broke out in late September 2000. For one thing, many Palestinians now pack rifles and even machine guns. Frequent armed attacks prompted Israeli forces to respond with heavier weapons than before, including tank and helicopter gunship fire. The televised conflict looked far more like actual warfare than the original uprising ever did. Meeting at a crisis summit in October, Arab leaders urged each other to sever all diplomatic ties with Israel. Such a move would effectively destroy peace treaties that Egypt and Jordan have with the world's only Jewish state. Iraq, Sudan, Libya, and Iran then called for an Islamic *jihad* to drive Israel's hated Jews into the sea. Muslims as far away as Pakistan and Indonesia—and even in London, New York, and Sydney—marched in support of the holy war call.

All of this seemingly turned the clock back some decades to the tumultuous days before the 1948, 1967, and 1973 Arab-Israeli wars. As the new millennium began to unfold, the smell in the sultry Middle East air was of a major battle ahead, centered on the holy city of Jerusalem. The sense that the battle was mainly centered on the city—sacred to Christians, Muslims, and even more so to Jews—was enhanced by the very name the Palestinians gave to their uprising, *Al-Aksa*. Muslims believe that Al-Aksa, meaning "the farthest place," refers to the site known to Christians and Jews as the Temple Mount in Jerusalem. The uprising's designated name seemed to reveal the true goal of the fresh revolt: to restore exclusive Islamic rule over the ancient, disputed holy site.

Exactly when we could see another large-scale regional war, which countries might be involved, and what the outcome is likely to be is included in the contents of this book. I did not just commence writing when the latest wave of violence began. Most of the material was already in my computer waiting for publication. The new uprising explosion prompted me to bring it out earlier than originally planned.

Coming almost exactly one year after the new uprising began here in Jerusalem, the outrageous and unprecedented Islamic suicide terrorist strikes on America have only increased the relevancy of this book. I not only examine the probable biblical contours of the next major Middle East war, but also spell out other prophetic events that are likely to follow it. With the United States, and indeed the whole world, joining Israel in a crisis that is very much rooted in this extremely troubled region, I believe that my work is all the more important for you to read and absorb.

The seminal inspiration to put *Israel in Crisis* into readers' hands came from a series of questions I am frequently asked when traveling and speaking around the world. The questions are mainly about modern Israel and the broader Middle East but also about how these historically rich areas relate to various biblical prophecies. I have strived to provide answers to many of these queries. I expect that you will find this book timely, informative, and even inspirational in places. I may be a professional journalist by training, but I am also a deep believer in Israel's sovereign Lord. This book reflects that fact as well, as I trust my life does every day.

1

The Final Ingathering

In my frequent travels to various parts of the world, several questions related to Israel and biblical prophecy recur. Although I am not a Bible scholar in any formal sense, I will attempt in this book to answer some of those questions based on my work as a Christian journalist living in Israel since 1980. Some of my views may not please every reader (I would be shocked if they did!), especially those who hold strong opinions on Israel and/or biblical prophecy. Nevertheless, I ask all to carefully consider the information and opinions that I present in the nondogmatic spirit in which they are offered.

The most fundamental question, frequently asked by Christian pastors and echoed by some of my local Arab acquaintances, is this humdinger: Is Israel's contemporary restoration as a nation *really* connected to ancient biblical prophecies? I was asked this for the umpteenth time only last week by a visiting German pastor here in Jerusalem. The underlying, but less often verbalized, query is this: How can modern Israel, with its secular Jewish majority, controversial policies, and seeming anti-Christian feelings, be in any way the fulfillment of prophetic promises made by God?

Such questions crop up even more frequently when actual fighting is going on between Israelis and Palestinians, meaning they are on the front burner once again in these crisis-filled days. The questions are often asked with intense passion, undoubtedly bolstered by televised images of the violent uprising. Israeli soldiers are clearly far more heavily armed than their Palestinian paramilitary counterparts, who do not (at least not yet) possess helicopter gunships, tanks, armored personnel carriers, and the like. A news camera positioned just right can capture the powerful visual contrast of helmeted, guntoting soldiers doing combat with stone- and firebomb-throwing youths. Such scenes, pitting the apparently powerful against the seemingly defenseless, evoke angry reactions from Palestinians and their allies around the world. They even bring up charges that the main victims of Hitler's holocaust, the Jews, are acting just like their former Nazi oppressors. News reports showing Israeli air-to-ground rockets and tank shells striking Palestinian positions near Bethlehem, in Jericho, in Ramallah north of Jerusalem, and in various parts of the Gaza Strip have further enhanced the widely held impression that the "Goliath" in this uprising conflict is mighty Israel, and the "David" is the Palestinian Arabs.

I have asked myself many times how the modern Jewish state could in any way be a fulfillment of biblical prophecy, especially when engaging in road combat with the numerous Israeli drivers who seemingly possess an enormous death wish, and while covering certain aspects of the Arab/Israeli conflict. Can a just and loving God really have anything to do with this fascinating yet ostensibly fairly godless state? Very much so, in my estimation. Having said that, I admit to my critics that my answer is more a product of faith than sight. Still, faith is the substance of things not yet seen, based on the Scriptures and the evident character and purposes of God.

I believe two portions of the Hebrew Bible (Old Testament to most Christian ears) are key to answering the above questions concerning Israel's dramatic reappearance, after a two thousand-year absence, on the crowded world stage. They are Ezekiel 36 and Isaiah 11. Let's take a look at Ezekiel first.

The prophet Ezekiel lived during the dreadful days of the first Jewish dispersion from the Promised Land. He tells us that he was "by the river Chebar among the exiles" (1:1) when he received his first revelation of Israel's exalted God. His people had been ripped away from their holy ground by the mighty Babylonian army. This was an initial fulfillment of God's repeated warnings, first delivered in the Sinai desert through Moses, that Jacob's descendants would be driven from their land if they committed grievous sins while living in it.

After several centuries of mostly bad government under corrupt kings and queens, and with religious idolatry thriving under false prophets and evil priests, the people were ripe for dispersion. They had already been divided by civil war, leading to the emergence of rival northern and southern kingdoms. Following decades of fierce battles, the northern kingdom was finally overwhelmed by Assyrian forces in 721 B.C. Crestfallen, the people were forcibly relocated to various parts of Nineveh's sprawling empire. But attempts by King Sennacherib to capture Jerusalem failed. Eventually, the

Babylonians succeeded where their predecessor had fallen short. Solomon's sacred temple—built around the year 950 B.C.—was finally destroyed in 587 after its treasures were carried off to Babylon.

The Bible tells us that the holy city remained under pagan Gentile control for about seventy years. Then, in accordance with prophecies delivered by Ezekiel and others, the territory first promised to Abraham was restored to its divinely appointed inhabitants by a merciful God acting through the beneficent King Cyrus. The temple and city were slowly rebuilt, as recorded in the books of Ezra and Nehemiah.

Israel's fortunes would ebb and flow until the coming of the promised Messiah, Yeshua, half a millennium later. Between periods of Jewish freedom and prosperity, European Greeks and Romans imposed their rule. By the time Yeshua was crucified by Roman soldiers at the behest of Israel's religious authorities, the end was near. Some forty years later, in A.D. 70, Herod's magnificent temple was destroyed and the Jewish people were dispersed from Jerusalem a second time. They were not only scattered to regions east of the Promised Land, but also to the north, south, and especially to the west. As the centuries of exile progressed, they literally wandered, or were driven to, the farthest reaches of the globe. Still they kept their unique, Holy Land–centered faith intact wherever they went.

Reflecting other biblical passages, Ezekiel records God as saying that the forced Jewish dispersion from the land was a *hillul ha shem,* a desecration of His name. This is especially made clear in Ezekiel 36:20: "When they came to the nations where they went, they profaned My holy name, because it was said of them, 'These are the people of the LORD; yet they have come out of His land.'"

Thus, the fact that Jews had been driven from their sanctified territory and were therefore found in significant numbers elsewhere, was a grave slap in God's face. If Israel's sovereign Lord—who claimed to be the *only* true God and Creator of all things—could not keep His chosen people safe in their own land, then maybe His assertions of exclusive divinity were bogus. If this deity had indeed said that the city of Jerusalem would be His unique resting place on earth, yet His Jewish people now turned their faces in prayer toward their *destroyed* temple from far-flung distant lands, then His self-professed power and assertions of unrivaled divinity were definitely called into question.

Fortunately for Israel, God's rebuke against His rebellious people is contained in a section of Scripture that speaks mainly of Jewish *restoration* to the land. Ezekiel is told to prophesy to the mountains of Israel, telling them that they will again "put forth your branches and bear your fruit for My people Israel; for they will soon come" (36:8).

Bearing in mind that Ezekiel was speaking in the midst of the Babylonian exile, the foretold return should naturally refer to the one fulfilled in the prophet's era. Indeed, many Jews did come back to their biblical heartland—the hills of Judea and Samaria, with Jerusalem nestled in between the two areas. But there are significant indications that the God of Israel, speaking to His people through the exiled seer, was also referring to a far off and final return to the land.

In verse 12, God tells the mountains that He will "cause men—My people Israel—to walk on you and possess you, so that you will become their inheritance and *never again* bereave them of children" (italics mine). In fact, the hallowed hills were once more made bereft of Jewish offspring after the Babylonian return, and not just for seventy years. The second, Roman dispersion

Israel in Crisis

lasted nearly two thousand years, beginning to be reversed only in the past century. Pockets of Jews remained in the sparsely populated regions of Judea and Samaria in the intervening years but not in the flourishing manner described in the previous verses.

The strongest indications that Ezekiel's prophecy was mainly referring to a final, much more significant ingathering comes in verses 24 through 31. After again rebuking His scattered people for their sin and unbelief in verse 23, God says, "I will . . . gather you from all the lands and bring you into your own land" in order to "sprinkle clean water on you" and to "cleanse you from all your filthiness and from all your idols." "Moreover," He says, "I will give you a new heart and put a new spirit within you; and I will remove the heart of stone from your flesh and give you a heart of flesh." In other words, God will not only cleanse them from their sin, but will also remove the old sinful heart—the fallen nature— from them.

Many Christian scholars argue, with good reason, that this cleansing in fact took place after the Babylonian return, in the person of the Messiah Jesus. His death and resurrection fulfilled the need for blood atonement and delivered new life to God's chosen people. This is certainly the case. Yet it is also a sad historic fact that many, if not most, Jews living in the land during the time of Christ rejected the Lord's atonement and thus did not receive the new heart prophesied in these intriguing passages of Scripture.

The strongest evidence that these verses are primarily speaking of a yet future occurrence is contained in verses 27 and 28. Not only will the Jewish remnant receive God's own Spirit within them, giving them the ability to keep all of His commandments; they will do so while *living in the land* that God says He "gave" to their forefathers. So we see that the promised new heart and spirit are directly connected to residing and flourishing in the literal Promised Land! That this "land" is not some ethereal place, but the actual hills, valleys, and ravines of Judea and Samaria (v. 6) is evident from the overall text. These verses also clearly state that God's spiritual gifts would be poured out in connection to a *permanent* Jewish foothold in the biblical heartland. If so, then the prophecy cannot be referring to the time of Messiah's incarnation, since the Jews were expelled from the hilly regions within decades of the Lord's death and resurrection.

For the third time in this section of Scripture, God tells the Jewish remnant very emphatically that He is not restoring them physically to the land and saving them spiritually because they deserve it. "'I am not doing this for your sake,' declares the Lord GOD, 'let it be known to you. Be ashamed and confounded for your ways, O house of Israel!'" (v. 32). I have quoted this passage on many occasions to Arab Christians and others who reject the contention that God has anything to do with the modern reborn Jewish state. As God clearly said through His prophet, He is not restoring His land to the Jewish people because they have earned such a gift, but because He is a covenant-keeping Sovereign who has regard for His own reputation.

The fact that the prophesied Jewish restoration and cleansing refer to something more than what occurred at Calvary is emphasized in the remaining verses of Ezekiel 36. The marvelous gifts God promises to give will be intricately connected to the rebuilding and inhabiting of Israel's cities and waste places (v. 33), to the point that the restored condition will strike foreigners as miraculous, ultimately resulting in something akin to the prehistoric Garden of Eden (v. 35). The surrounding nations will apparently go through some sort of upheaval during this restoration process, causing them to finally recognize that it is the Lord Himself who has "rebuilt the ruined places and planted that which was desolate" (v. 36). At that time, the once-destroyed cities will overflow with inhabitants.

The Jewish return from the relatively short stay in Babylon did indeed lead to the rebuilding of many decimated towns and cities. But it was nothing compared to what has been occurring in our time, as I have personally witnessed for more than twenty years. Jewish communities in the mountains of Judea and Samaria like Bethel, Shilo, and Tekoa simply ceased to exist for almost twenty centuries. But they, and many other biblical places, have all been rebuilt in our era, along with other towns outside of the mountains, like Arad, Beer Sheba, Beit Shean, and Beit Shemesh. And then there is Jerusalem, a forlorn backwater for many centuries but now a thriving metropolis with more than six hundred thousand residents (including me). The fact that modern Israel is becoming one of the most densely populated places on earth is also significant in light of the prophecy that God will increase the Jewish presence "like a flock" (v. 37).

Ezekiel 37

Israel's physical return in unbelief and subsequent spiritual rebirth in the land is expanded upon in Ezekiel 37. This is the famous "dry bones" vision known to Sunday school children around the world. Ezekiel sees a valley filled with decaying, dry bones. God then asks him if it is possible for such bones to live again. After Ezekiel acknowledges that only God knows, he is told that the bones will indeed be covered by sinews and flesh once more. Then this miraculously takes place.

The prophet notes, however, that while the bones are covered with sinews, flesh, and skin, there is "no breath in them" (v. 8). Ezekiel is then instructed to prophesy to the breath (Hebrew *ruach*, the same word for spirit) to come and fill "these slain, that they come to life" (v. 9). While this could refer to the general resurrection of the dead spoken of elsewhere in Scripture, or of the final resurrection of saved Jewish people, it fits the context best to principally interpret it as the physical rebirth of annihilated Israel. If so, then we have another picture of the historical restoration (flesh and bones) occurring first, followed by the spiritual infilling.

Ezekiel's prophecies teach us something else: We need not be too concerned if today's "average Israeli" is not exactly the epitome of holiness. Ezekiel 36 is explicit and unequivocal that the prophesied Jewish renewal will *follow* an actual return to, and upbuilding of, the Promised Land. Since the contemporary ingathering is so much more widespread and dramatic than the first one—with several million Jews literally coming to live in Israel from over one hundred countries in every part of the globe—the present restoration must surely at least be the preliminary fulfillment of God's exciting, solemn promises.

Again, it must be stressed that Israel's incredible rebirth, with its resurrected language, agriculture, government and religious institutions, and so on, is not due to any merit on the part of the scattered Jewish people. Nor is it primarily the result of Britain, the United Nations, or America. It is an act of grace, coming from Israel's gracious Father. More than this, God has not welcomed the shame heaped upon His divine reputation due to the Jewish dispersion and is largely acting to remove that blight. In light of the fact that this is repeated no less than three times in Ezekiel's prophecy (36:21–22, 32), no Christian or Jew who believes in the veracity of the Scriptures should have any reason to doubt God's involvement in—nay, responsibility for—the contemporary Jewish return to and restoration of Zion.

Although I'm not thrilled to do so, I have no biblical problem confessing Israel's numerous sins while traveling outside the country. The fact that my Jewish neighbors generally fail to act like born-again Christians is no surprise to me, since they are not born again (apart from a tiny minority). Most at least do not claim to be especially holy, in contrast to many evangelical Christians (including yours truly at times) whose actions belie their born-again professions.

Since Ezekiel foretold that scattered Jews would return in unbelief and later receive their new heart and spirit in the land, I am not overly bothered that nascent Israel does not always reflect the highest moral standards. The Bible records in many places that spiritual salvation will come to regathered Israel in the *last days*, in the midst of a world conflagration that comes to a climax in and over rebuilt Jerusalem. In the meantime, the world's only Jewish country is like all others, except that none has such a glorious future foretold for it.

Since the Bible records that the Jewish people were expelled from God's special land because of their numerous sins, do they deserve a state today? Considering their seemingly unparalleled historic suffering, the strictly humanitarian answer is certainly yes. But, biblically speaking, probably not. God's answer, revealed through Ezekiel, is a definite no. Yet God nevertheless promised to restore them to His land *for His name's sake* and for the sake of some of their pious forebears. More than this, He is doing it because He is a merciful, covenant-keeping God. Can professing Christians, no matter how anti-Zionist, be unhappy that we are saved by a covenant-keeping God who forgives sins?

Some Christian scholars and leaders have been put off from supporting the above position after exposure to overzealous "Christian Zionists." Indeed, some of my pro-Israel brethren both here and abroad have definitely appeared to be "more Catholic than the pope," or should we say, "more Jewish than the chief rabbis." The state of Israel can seemingly do no wrong in their estimation. Recognizing some of the apparent flaws of this re-emerging nation (I can present a fairly full list, but why confess other people's sins?), many Christian scholars and leaders have simply chucked the Israeli baby out with the bath water. That is a tragic mistake and a shame, in my estimation, since the Jewish return to the land I call home shouts to the heavens of the reality and faithfulness of Israel's God.

Isaiah 11

The above is my answer to the many questions and objections I receive concerning Israel's current national manifestation. But another related question has arisen in recent years, due to the teachings of several prominent Jewish and Gentile believers. Might Israel be forced to endure yet another exile in our time and then a subsequent third return to the land? Those who think the answer is maybe, or a definite yes, point to the very sins to which I have alluded above.

I am convinced that while Israel may suffer great hardships in the future, as many prophecies indicate, the teaching that the state might be totally destroyed is an unbiblical notion. The Scriptures certainly demonstrate that God judges the sins of nations. Still, are Israel's moral failings any worse than other countries built on Judeo-Christian values, such as England and America? Not in the least, in my informed opinion (speaking as an American journalist who has covered this pulsating land for many years, and as a frequent visitor to Europe and the United States). Nonetheless, God will surely deal with Israeli Jews in His time and manner, as He will with Gentile nations.

The question of Israel's potential third dispersion is dealt with in Isaiah 11. This chapter contains the fullest prophetic description of what the world will be like when the promised Messiah, the Offspring of David, comes to rule and reign in rebuilt Jerusalem.

Who cannot but cherish the promise that a time will come when the ravenous "wolf will dwell with the lamb, and the leopard will lie down with the kid . . . and a little boy will lead them" (v. 6)? Who cannot but glow in anticipation for a future where the Lord will rule the world with incorruptible justice and overflowing wisdom (vv. 2–4)? Who does not long for a time when there will no longer be any war or violence upon this weary, blood-soaked planet (v. 9)?

Isaiah tells us exactly when this heavenly vision will become reality on earth. The Messiah's second coming will occur in tandem with a second Jewish return to the beloved Promised Land! This is revealed in verse 11:

> Then it will happen on that day that the Lord
> Will again recover the *second time* with His hand
> The remnant of His people who will remain,
> From Assyria, Egypt, Pathros, Cush, Elam Shinar,
>   Hamath,
> And from the islands of the sea (italics mine).

Who is the remnant of His people spoken of here? Is it the largely Gentile church? Is it the Jehovah's Witnesses or some other sect? Or is it the Jewish people? And when will all this take place?

defend our + others' freedom.
This lie of Satan is being
promoted to destroy everything
you + I hold dear. There is no
proof to support Global warming
+ Al Gore's film is full of lies +
distortions. You need to get informed.
You would be wise to read Michael Coffman's
book "Saviors of the Earth?", which
exposes who + what, including the
New Age spiritual forces that are worship of Gaia,
behind this Satanic deception.
It is part of the end times plan to
bring us into the "one World Order",
Satanic government. And
∴ you have made yourself an
instrument of our enemy, Satan.
"With what harmony is there between
Christ and Belial (a worthless, lawless
person)?" "Do not be unequally
yoked."
∴ I can no longer support CBN.
because you are deceived + thus contributing
to the deception of others.

I am Appalled! that
you have publicly aligned
yourself w/ such ~~despicable~~
~~Al Gore~~ colossial liars +
deceivers as Al Sharpton, Al
Gore + Ted Turner. It shocks +
amazes me. For you to align
yourself in a public commercial
w/ Sharpton + ~~Gore~~ is grievous.
You are grievously misinformed,
uninformed + ignorant of the
facts re global warming. It is
a sham and a scam being
perpetrated ~~that~~ upon the Amer. public in
order to destroy this nation's
economy + bring us into 3rd
world status ~~+ longer~~ so we will
no longer be a super power able to

Verse 12 clarifies that the physical descendants of Jacob are being spoken of here, not the Gentile church or some other entity:

> And He will lift up a standard for the nations,
> And will assemble the banished ones of Israel,
> And will gather the dispersed of Judah
> From the four corners of the earth.

Of course, Jacob's progeny are today mostly referred to as "Jews," a name that comes directly from the tribe of Judah, from which the Messiah came. This is not the church or some non-Jewish sect heading home to some mystical Zion in the sky. It is the offspring of Jacob literally returning to their sanctified land *for a second time* in history.

Some argue that the current ingathering is not the second historical return but the third. This is based on the notion that the exodus from Egypt was the first one and thus the Babylonian return the second. Although not a "licensed" biblical scholar by any means, I cannot agree with this premise. The Bible clearly records that Jacob's sons and their families were not exiled to Egypt but headed southwest on their own accord. The relatively small band was not forced out of the Promised Land but willingly left to secure food in a time of severe drought. Thus, the miracle-filled return some four hundred years later was not an ingathering from exile. Indeed, under Joshua's leadership, it was actually the initial conquest of most sections of the land that God promised Abraham He would give to the patriarch's descendants.

The ancient Israelis (Israelites in biblical English) were not regathered to what had been their own territory. In the time of Jacob, the land housed several different peoples, of which Abraham's seed were but one. The Jews did not become a nation ruling over most of the Promised Land until after the time of Joshua. Time-wise, this clearly followed their sojourn in Egypt. So the displacement that began with the Assyrian conquest and continued under the Babylonian expulsions was the first exile for the Jewish nation, and the Roman dispersion was the second. Therefore, the current return is also the second one foretold in Isaiah 11:11.

Some scholars maintain that the phrase "the second time" implies that there will be two distinct Jewish regatherings from the four corners of the earth, and therefore the current return will end in another mass expulsion from the Promised Land. Having an ability to read the original text in Hebrew, I find this contention untenable as well. Isaiah could have easily said "the Lord will recover *two times* with His hand." Indeed, there exists an exact Hebrew word, *pamime*, that clearly expresses this. Instead, the verse contains the word *shaineet*, which means "a second time" or "a second occasion." In other words, this prophecy is about the second ingathering, which will be from all over the globe. The Hebrew text does not at all imply that the Jews will *twice* be scattered from their land to the farthest reaches of the planet. The details that follow simply amplify the second ingathering foretold in verse 11.

When will Messiah's righteous kingdom—with its radical transformation of the wild animal kingdom and of even wilder human nature—be made fully manifest on earth? Isaiah 11:11 says it will come "on that day," or in the same general time frame, as the second Jewish regathering to the ancient biblical homeland. In other words, Israel's second return to national life on the world stage is the sign of all signs that the Lord's second coming is drawing near. That should be enough to make anyone a "Christian Zionist"!

I am also sometimes asked a related question. What percentage of scattered world Jewry will return before the Lord appears in the clouds? Again, I am not technically qualified to answer that. But as a close observer of modern Israel, I do wager an opinion. It will be at least 40 percent, since that is the approximate number already living here, with new immigrants arriving every day. Will it be 100 percent? In other words, do all the Jews have to return home to Israel before the Lord can come back to rule in Jerusalem? There is no biblical reason to say so. In fact, the opposite seems to be the case. Ezekiel 39:27 indicates that the Lord will complete the Jewish ingathering only *after* He vanquishes His enemies and begins to rule on earth.

This brings up a final related question. Could the current, ongoing Jewish migration be merely a phantom? In other words, might Israel's reconstitution as a nation after two thousand years of exile be of little or no significance, with the relevant final return still entirely ahead? Some have taken this position. I believe, however, that this proposition is extremely untenable, especially in light of Ezekiel's prophetic word that Jacob's children would come back "without the spirit" to their sacred land and only here be dealt with by the Almighty.

I personally cannot believe that Israel's omniscient God would apparently deceive His largely Gentile bride on earth by allowing almost half of world Jewry to move back to the Galilee, to the hills and valleys of Judea and Samaria, to the fertile coastal plane, and to the Negev desert if this return had no biblical significance. More than this, Israel's reappearance after such a long absence cannot be a malicious act of Satan, as some Arab Christians and others maintain. The Bible states emphatically that God rules over the affairs of men, especially the establishment and destruction of nations. In that sense at least, Israel's rebirth is indisputably an act of God.

One fact is undeniable: After two thousand years of exile, a large portion of the dispersed, despised, persecuted offspring of Israel live once again inside their ancient ancestral boundaries. It is not some psychological fantasy or freaky acid trip, even if Yasser Arafat and many others might wish it were. It is concrete and steel reality. How we interpret Israel's reemergence on the world stage is one thing. But no one can dispute that a literal banner has been lifted up in our time for the entire world to see, as the prophet Isaiah foretold (v. 12). That banner is a flag widely recognized around the world and patterned after a Jewish prayer shawl. In its center is an ancient symbol associated with King David, the Messiah's progenitor. If all this is biblically insignificant, then I am the monkey's uncle my high school biology teacher indicated I am.

2

The Last Generation

===

Is Israel's national reappearance a sign that the prophesied end of the age is fast approaching? This is the position taken by many popular Christian writers. It is also a question I'm frequently asked while traveling abroad. I believe the biblical answer is yes, although I base my response not so much on the usual sources, such as the Olivet Discourse delivered by Yeshua at the beginning of His final week in Jerusalem. I base my reply mainly on a psalm, one that seems to connect Israel's national restoration with the Holocaust of World War II.

Israel's modern advent can be described as miraculous in several ways. No other people have lost their sovereignty for such a long period of time and then reemerged as a flourishing nation. If the odds are overwhelmingly negative that an ancient people group could return to vibrant national life in their former boundaries after being scattered all over the earth for nineteen centuries, what are they if that particular racial group just happens to be one of the most demonized in history? Yet this is the story of the Jewish people. It is not a fairy tale; it is gruesome reality.

Miracles are not always painless. Indeed, they are acts of God that often come in the midst of great suffering. Such is clearly the case with Israel's extraordinary national rebirth—out of the flames of Adolf Hitler's hideous Nazi Holocaust.

While generally agreeing that there was at least a touch of the miraculous in their decimated country's modern restitution, many Israelis object to the Christian propensity to link Hitler's genocidal program with Israel's subsequent reappearance on the world map. I understand their objections. The backbreaking groundwork for their state was accomplished in the decades before the second world war, mostly by dedicated men and women who were not overtly religious. The 1922 League of Nations mandate authorized Britain to oversee the establishment of a Jewish homeland in the biblical Holy Land. The United Nations voted in 1947 to include the emerging state in the list of recognized nations. Both acts were largely the fruit of intensive work by the international Zionist movement. Israel's rebirth was not merely a vote of sympathy following the Holocaust, but a well-earned reward for decades of Jewish sweat and blood in the Promised Land.

Still, it is an indisputable fact that a shocked world was just waking up to the magnitude of Nazi atrocities as the UN was gearing up to vote on "the question of Palestine." Thus, anguished sympathy for the horrendous Jewish loss, and shame over widespread Gentile acquiescence to it, must have contributed to the overwhelming UN vote to support the establishment of a sovereign Jewish state. Indeed, several countries who voted yes testified that this was the case.

Psalm 102

I am convinced that the Bible itself links Israel's national resurrection with the Nazi Holocaust—and also with the end of this age. This link comes not in the writings of one of Israel's anointed biblical prophets, but in an anonymous psalm. Let me explain.

Reuvan Ross, an American-born Jewish friend, held a small weekly Bible study in the south Jerusalem neighborhood of Gilo in the late 1980s. Three other men and myself attended (two went on to become messianic pastors here in the city). Reuvan emphasized over and over again the importance of spending quality time *every day* with the Lord, praying and studying His Word. While this was already an important part of my life, it was not always a *daily* part. Aside from the rare, upside-down travel day or days featuring an unexpected terror attack or other breaking news, I have kept my daily appointment ever since.

It was during one of those divine morning meetings that an ancient psalm struck me like a *Luftwaffe* bomb falling from the sky. I had only recently seen *Schindler's List* for the first time. The film's graphic and harrowing images—the gas showers, the spewing smokestacks, the endless ash from emaciated, burning bodies, the massacres, the screams of terror, the piles of human bones—were still fresh in my memory.

"This is a prophecy about Hitler's Holocaust!" I exclaimed as I read through the first portion of Psalm 102. Such was news to me, as it might be to you.

31

Steven Spielberg's Oscar-winning film brought floods of tears to many theaters across the globe. Nowhere was that more the case than here in Israel. Movie seats were filled with many sobbing people who had somehow survived the genocidal slaughter, or with relatives, friends, or acquaintances of both the spared and slain victims. To Israeli audiences, it was an extremely personal film about an unmitigated disaster that had struck their extended family. Profuse weeping and a number of early exits testified to this. To say the least, it was an especially traumatic experience to watch the torturously realistic film here in the Jewish homeland.

I had always heard from Jewish friends that the Bible was silent on what was probably history's most grotesque mass civilian slaughter. I found that assertion rather odd, since the Holy Book is mainly about the Jewish people, including their collective future. Still, I passively accepted the prevailing view. Of course, many attribute God's perceived silence to the ostensible "fact" that there is no heavenly "Keeper of Israel." I have heard this argument more than once while talking to Holocaust survivors or their relatives. Such people say that if God exists, He could not have allowed such a thing to take place, certainly not to His chosen people.

So, in a certain sense, it was actually comforting to discover that the Bible is not silent about this unrivaled black hole in Jewish history. Although God did not by any means cause it—the wicked hearts of fallen human beings did that—the omniscient Creator knew in advance that a genocidal disaster would one day befall His beloved covenant people. More than this, He heard the desperate prayers uttered by them in their anguished imprisonment. In answering them, He even brought some good out of this most terrible tragedy.

Indeed, the Hebrew word for the Holocaust—*shoah*—says it all. It connotes a "sacrifice." Like smoke rising from the holy temple, the colossal Jewish pain and suffering would ascend up to God, and He would transform it into new life. The shed blood of martyred Jews would act as a nutrient to help bring the olive tree of Israel back to life. While this concept may be objectionable to some who understandably insist that no good could have come from such a mass slaughter, it is nevertheless a historic fact.

Living for many years in Israel, I have heard countless messages based on portions of Psalm 102, but they have always focused on the middle section, verses 12 through 17. The rest of the psalm usually has been ignored.

The middle section foretells that the compassion of God would return one day to Zion. This would happen at a foreordained time in history, culminating in the Lord's glorious appearance. We are not told in Psalm 102 when or why God's mercy had previously been cut off; other parts of the Bible reveal that. We are only informed that His tender compassion toward His chosen city will be restored in the future at an "appointed time" (v. 13). The psalmist then prophesies that this divine act will cause the nations and their rulers to fear the Lord (v. 15).

Local preachers, delivering their messages in the pulsating modern city of Jerusalem, maintain that the "appointed time" apparently came in 1948, when the Jewish state, with part of Jerusalem as its capital, was reborn. They usually add that another peak was reached in 1967 when Israeli forces gained control of Judaism's holiest site on earth, the sacred Temple Mount with its revered Western Wall.

Although my Arab friends tend to disagree, I firmly believe that the many messages I've heard on this topic are biblically correct. Judaism's deep and enduring connection to Jerusalem is not of Jewish design. The Bible foretold that God Himself would choose a special place for His name to dwell on earth, later revealing that place to be the small Judean town of Jerusalem. During nineteen centuries of exile, Jewish prayers about the vanquished city and temple were recited daily. They were uttered by pious Jews facing toward the earthly Zion from Cairo, Athens, Rome, London, Moscow, New York, Buenos Aires, Sydney, Cape Town—you name it, they were probably there. Penitent Jews were calling upon their eternal Father to have compassion on Jerusalem by returning His chosen children to it.

That the central section of Psalm 102 is not referring to some heavenly, ethereal Zion is made clear in verse 14: "Surely Thy servants find pleasure in her stones, and feel pity for her dust." This is not some celestial icon, but a down-to-earth place full of stones and dust and by inference few natural water sources. This is the actual city of Jerusalem, located amid the dry and dusty hills of Judea in the semiarid Middle East.

The city I call home is today a place where most buildings, by law, must be faced by off-white Jerusalem stones. Authorities decided to enforce this rule, since the stones, or more often stone slabs, give the modern city an ancient, timeless, and quite intriguing look. When the skies are blue and the sun bright, as on most days, the city glows with brilliant light. When the sun rises in the east, the buildings normally display a pinkish tint. When it sets in the west, all of Jerusalem reflects its golden hues. I suspect that a second reason why city officials made the use of Jerusalem stones mandatory is that they knew we had better do something constructive with them lest they become weapons in the latest battle!

How does all this connect to the Jewish Holocaust? As stated earlier, Psalm 102 does not begin with stirring verses about God's compassion on Jerusalem and the

Lord's subsequent appearance in the city. Israel's rebirth did not happen in a vacuum. It occurred in the immediate wake of the worst war in human history. It followed on the heels of bloodied Nazi jackboots, forever stained with buckets of Jewish blood.

I strongly believe that verses 1 through 11 speak of that dreadful period of world and Jewish history. When I came to that conclusion, I had never heard this taught by anyone. As I said, it occurred to me while reading Psalm 102 soon after viewing *Schindler's List*. I've since learned of several Christian professors and preachers who have come to the same conclusion.

A number of key words in verses 3 through 9 leaped out at me as I read through the familiar psalm on that mild morning. But let's begin at the beginning. Verses 1 and 2 make clear that the psalmist is experiencing tremendous adversity. In a "day of distress" he cries out to God for help, urging Him to quickly intervene. Then come the first of the key words: "For my days have been consumed *in smoke,* and my bones have been *scorched* like a hearth" (v. 3, italics mine). What an odd thing to say. Somehow, the psalmist's distressing days feature smoke, and it is apparently coming from his own burning bones! Who does not know today that some of Hitler's death camps contained crematoria where bodies were burned to ash? I have visited one of them in Austria.

The King James Version mistranslates this as "my days are consumed *like* smoke" (italics mine). But the original Hebrew is quite clear. The word for smoke, *ashan,* is preceded by the Hebrew letter *bet,* which usually means "in" or sometimes "on," but rarely "like."

Verses 4 through 7 focus on the debilitating effects of starvation. The psalmist says his heart has "withered away," because, in his great anguish, he "forgets to eat" his bread (v. 4). Amid loud groaning, he reports, "My

35

bones cling to my flesh" (v. 5). Who has not seen photographs of the many emaciated concentration camp victims? Indeed, the main cause of death at the German Buchenwald camp was starvation. This theme is continued in verses 6 and 7. The writer likens himself to a lonesome owl that stays awake all night, unable to sleep due to hunger and despair.

Verses 8 and 9 fully convinced me that I was not just imagining a parallel between the Holocaust and this ancient psalm. In verse 8 of the version I was reading (the New American Standard Bible), the translators have accurately rendered a Hebrew phrase into English, while assigning the literal wording to the margin notes. The NASB says, "My enemies have reproached me all day long; those who deride me *have used my name as a curse*" (italics mine).

The Hebrew literally reads, "My enemies . . . *have sworn by me.*" Therefore, the King James Version says, "They that are mad against me are sworn against me." The NASB translators, however, obviously understood that the original words in Hebrew can form an expression meaning, "my very own name has been used as a curse against me."

Did any such thing happen during World War II? All should know that answer. Jews throughout Nazi-occupied Europe and North Africa were forced to wear a yellow star on their clothing. It was patterned after an ancient six-sided symbol connected to Israel's exalted King David. The Jewish prophets foretold that the Messiah would come from Judah, David's family tribe. The yellow stars had the name "Jude" printed on them. This is the modern name of the ancient Hebrews—Jew—derived from the tribe of Judah. Did the "Star of David" badge therefore signify that "Christian Germany" was honoring the Messiah's racial cousins, recognizing that the bloodline of contemporary Jews is exactly the same as Christ's? Honor was hardly the word.

Verse 9 contains another unusual phrase that hearkens to the Holocaust: "For I have *eaten ashes* like bread, and mingled my drink with weeping" (italics mine). Spielberg's famous film also portrayed this gut-wrenching aspect of many of the death camps. The ashen remains of cremated bodies billowed out of towering camp chimneys, only to rain back down onto the camps when the winds were contrary. Thus, inmates were sometimes forced to breathe in, and even taste, the sooty remains of their fellow Jews.

The psalmist goes on to acknowledge that God has had at least an indirect hand in his horrendous sufferings: "Because of Thine indignation and Thy wrath; for Thou hast lifted me up and cast me away" (v. 10). In other words, none of his harsh experiences could have taken place if God had not allowed them to. Note that he does not state that God is *responsible* for his sufferings, but only that they are the result of the Lord's taking away His protective covering in righteous anger.

As the Scriptures warn elsewhere, repeated and unrepentant sin can cause a holy God to turn His face away from us, leaving His frail creatures to make their lonely way along humanity's warped paths while battling Satan's cruel intentions. Does this mean every Holocaust sufferer was an evil sinner? Certainly no more than anyone else who has lived on earth. Among the victims were many young children and those who truly loved and served God. It only indicates that the underlying reason such a thing could take place was the overarching presence of human sin, evil, and rebellion against God.

This rather depressing section of Psalm 102 concludes in verse 11. The unknown author bemoans the fact that he is "withering away like grass." Nothing seems to lie ahead of him but death and oblivion.

If the psalm ended at this point, it would be gut-wrenching reading indeed. But suddenly the tone completely changes to one of optimism, hope, and praise for the Almighty. The preceding intense suffering will somehow be connected to the glorious redemption of the Jewish people and the restoration of their beloved homeland!

Verse 12 begins with an acknowledgment of God's eternal nature: "But Thou, O Lord, dost abide forever; and Thy name to all generations." In other words, I may personally perish, but you won't do so. You will still be around to pick up the pieces, to put your people back together again, to restore and heal.

Now comes the famous verse 13:

> Thou wilt arise and have compassion on Zion;
> For it is time to be gracious to her,
> For the appointed time has come.

This preordained time of mercy upon Jerusalem is not going to occur out of the blue. It follows, and is intimately connected to, the unimaginable suffering that precedes it. But restoration and mercy will come, for it has long ago been set in Jerusalem stone by the Holy One of Israel.

What does all this have to do with the question that I posed at the beginning of this chapter: Is Israel's rebirth as a sovereign nation a sign of the end of days? The awesome answer is revealed in verses 16 and 18.

We saw in Ezekiel 36 that the Jewish exile from Jerusalem caused the nations to doubt the power and veracity of Israel's God. If their dispersion to all parts of the globe was a desecration of the Lord's good name, then their return to Zion is the opposite, a sanctification of that name. So the physical upbuilding of Jerusalem by the Jewish people is concrete proof that the self-proclaimed God of Israel is indeed God and still rules over human affairs. And when the nations witness that physical restoration in history, they should get ready for the Messiah-King to return to His holy city: "For the LORD has built up Zion; He has appeared in His glory" (v. 16).

Some might legitimately ask why verse 16 is suddenly in the past tense, when the preceding verses of Psalm 102 are clearly about the *future* restoration of Zion. This question obviously bothered the King James translators, who transformed it into a matching future-tense verse: "When the LORD shall build up Zion, he shall appear in his glory." But the NASB is faithful here to the original Hebrew, which suddenly switches in verse 16 to the past tense.

I believe this is an example of what some Bible scholars have dubbed "the prophetic tense." In other words, the thing foretold here, although still future, is so certain to occur that the writer records it as if it has already taken place. Indeed, when the world sees downtrodden and forlorn Jerusalem (described as a forgotten relic of history by visiting author Mark Twain in the mid–1800s) being restored to its former glory, then it is time to begin looking up, for the Savior of the world is drawing nigh!

When humanity literally sees the seemingly God-forsaken, literal city of Jerusalem springing back to life; when it becomes the center of Jewish existence once again and of international attention; when it has one of the world's largest foreign press corps residing in it; when it is bursting forth with new schools, parks, cultural centers, roads, and religious institutions—all underneath the shadow of towering building cranes—then the Lord will be preparing to appear in His glory!

The restoration of Zion, in accordance with God's loving compassion, is now linked by the psalmist to his earlier recitations of woe: "He has regarded the prayer of the destitute, and has *not despised* their prayer" (v. 17, italics mine). In other words, Israel's Maker was not sleeping or on vacation when His covenant Jewish people went through the harrowing Holocaust flames. He was listening to their prayers, and He answered them— maybe not right away, maybe not in the way everyone would have liked, but He answered them nonetheless.

God's response was to return His despised and persecuted Jewish people back to their ancestral homeland, where they could multiply in relative safety and defend themselves with the same armed forces and other governmental means that their tormentors possessed. In doing so, verse 20 states that God was answering the prayers of a *groaning prisoner,* setting free one who was doomed to death. So this stirring psalm reflects the anguished pleas of a *prisoner!*

Sadly, not all Holocaust-era prisoners walked away from Hitler's death camps. Millions of Jews and others were slaughtered inside their dreaded walls and fences. But the Jewish people as a whole, including some of their progeny, were set free—to return to national sovereignty and religious fulfillment in Zion!

Now comes the kicker. In the original Hebrew, verse 18 states emphatically that Psalm 102 is especially written for one specific generation, and that generation will be *the final one of history!*

The King James Version, along with most others, including the NASB, mistranslates this verse as follows: "This shall be written for the generation to come: and the people which shall be created shall praise the Lord." However, the Hebrew does not say "coming generation," but *last* generation. The phrase in Hebrew is *l'dor acharon.* All Hebrew dictionaries agree that *acharon* means "last" or "final." A variation of that word, *acheret,* means "coming" or "another."

So why did the English language translators, even of the normally literal NASB, apparently wimp out here? (The NASB doesn't even give the literal Hebrew translation in its margin, as it usually does in such cases.) The implications of the actual Hebrew phrase are enormous. One could translate verse 18 in a flowing manner as follows: "This prophecy is being specifically written for the final generation of human history. It will only make full sense to that generation, the one able to read about these things not just in this psalm, but also in their daily newspapers."

In summary, there would be only one particular generation in history that could pick up a book like the one you are holding now and read portions of this ancient psalm and then have the author explain precisely where and when many of the futuristic verses were fulfilled. That generation—yet to be created at the time when the psalm was recorded—would "praise the Lord" in a special way. Their praise would result from widespread recognition that Jerusalem's anointed King was building up His dusty city before their very eyes, preparing to return to the Mount of Olives in regal splendor.

But what is a biblical generation? Hal Lindsey said forty years. Others say less, some more. In the Book of Genesis, it is foretold that the children of Israel would be "strangers in Egypt" for 430 years. Then in the *fourth generation* they would return to the Promised Land (15:16). So according to that reckoning, a generation could be just over one hundred years! But often in the Bible it is calculated as the usual human life span, about seventy years.

However we reckon a biblical generation, Psalm 102 seems to foretell the following: At a certain point in history there would exist a group of people who would witness the Holocaust, the restoration of Jerusalem as a thriving Jewish center, and the coming of the Lord to reign in the holy city. Two out of three so far ain't bad!

Thus, this is the portion of Scripture that I refer to when people ask me if Israel's modern rebirth is a sign that the prophesied end of the age is at hand. In my humble opinion, the bustling city that I have called home since 1984 is the sign of all signs that the Lord's return in glory is almost visible on the eastern horizon. As some of my Jewish friends say, may the promised Messiah come speedily in our day!

3

The Sign of Jerusalem

During my initial years as a born-again Christian, *The Late Great Planet Earth* was one of the best-selling books in America. Hal Lindsey's apocalyptic thriller perfectly fit the recession-plagued 1970s. Another book, this one nonreligious, also sold well during that nervous decade. Written by Jonathan Schell, *The Fate of the Earth* gripped many readers with its vision of pending nuclear war and ecological disaster. Almost everybody in America, whether Christian or not, seemed to be anticipating doomsday. A sense of foreboding also prevailed in much of the rest of the globe.

Fears of imminent disaster spilled over into the early 1980s. Billy Graham came out with a book in 1981 titled *Till Armageddon.* Although it mainly dealt with the topic of suffering, the inside jacket provocatively asked, "What will it take to survive the personal turmoils, economic chaos, the dangerous world political climate now emerging on a scale perhaps unparalleled in human history?"

Such questions definitely fit the time. The powerful Soviet military had invaded Afghanistan in late 1979, setting off another long proxy war with the United States. In neighboring Iran, fifty-two Americans had been taken hostage in the besieged U.S. embassy by Iranian Muslim militants bent on spreading their violent revolution to the rest of the globe. The world economy was in a slump. About the only good news of that period was the signing of the Camp David peace accord between Egypt and Israel. Still, many expected the power-crazed Kremlin, which fiercely opposed the agreement, to send its forces marching toward the Middle East at virtually any moment.

The depths of doom and gloom in America were reached in 1983 when the ABC television network aired a terrifying movie titled *The Day After.* With stark realism, it bleakly portrayed a Soviet nuclear attack on the U.S. heartland. Very few people slept easily the night it was aired, for all realized such a destructive war with the "evil empire" was entirely possible.

But Armageddon didn't come. The Afghan war would be the giant Soviet bear's last hurrah. The American hostages were released. The global economy greatly improved (apart from the recession that followed the Wall Street stock slide of late 1987). Dictators were toppled. The Iron Curtain came down. Superpower nuclear weapons stockpiles were reduced. Cable television and the Internet helped spread information and democratic ideals around the globe like never before. By the time the new century dawned, the end of the world seemed like the theme of an old horror flick.

But there was one stark interruption to the global party. The 1990s began with a reminder that the Middle East is still a very explosive part of God's green earth. Still, the U.S.-led romp over Iraq only demonstrated that the collapsing Soviet Union was no longer a serious threat, leaving technologically advanced Washington and its European allies alone on top of the world.

OSLO PEACE ACCORD

Amid the nuclear-free, roaring prosperity of the swinging 90s, few American Christians or even believers in less-prosperous countries seemed to notice that a vital piece of the end-time puzzle spoken of by Hal Lindsey, Billy Graham, and others was finally falling into place. That vital piece was Jerusalem.

Ironically, the essential piece of the prophetic end-time puzzle has been moving into its prophesied position because of peace! It was the U.S. and Russian–sponsored Arab-Israeli "peace process" of the 1990s that led to important prophetic movement concerning Jerusalem. In particular, it was Israel's written commitment to *negotiate the status* of her most sacred city that really set the last days' ball rolling.

That commitment came as part of secret negotiations conducted in Oslo, Norway, in 1993. The clandestine talks were heartily supported by the new Clinton administration. As Egyptian President Anwar Sadat had done at Camp David in 1978, PLO leader Yasser Arafat demanded that Israel agree to formally discuss the final status of Jerusalem. He wanted the talks to especially focus on the walled Old City, which the Muslim world desperately wants returned to Islamic sovereignty. Jimmy Carter was able to persuade Sadat and Israeli Prime Minister Menachem Begin to agree to postpone the issue to a later stage of the peace process. Bill Clinton didn't even try, realizing that the explosive topic could no longer be deflected.

In my 1998 book, *Israel at the Crossroads,* I explained why I thought peace talks over Jerusalem would ultimately fail. The quick summary is this: The city contains Judaism's holiest sites on earth. After centuries of separation from it, the Israelis will never cede formal sovereignty over the Old City and surrounding areas as demanded by the entire Arab world. Any leader who dared to do so would provoke serious civil strife and probably end up assassinated like Oslo accord signer Yitzhak Rabin. Israeli Prime Minister Ehud Barak made this point at the failed Camp David summit meeting with President Clinton and Yasser Arafat in July 2000.

On the Arab side, Jerusalem is also a religious issue at its heart. Although not Islam's holiest site on earth, the Muslim "Noble Sanctuary" (Temple Mount) is *the place* where Islam's self-proclaimed superiority over Christianity and Judaism was demonstrated many centuries ago for all to see. The very veracity and honor of the Muslim holy book, the Koran, is called into question by a Jewish state holding sovereignty over the Noble Sanctuary, along with other sacred Islamic sites in Hebron and elsewhere. Any Arab leader who did not secure full Muslim control over eastern Jerusalem's Old City in a final peace accord would also be a prime candidate to share Rabin's bloody fate. Yasser Arafat pointed this out to Clinton and Barak at Camp David, saying it was the main reason he would have to refuse Barak's rather generous concessions on Jerusalem. He said the compromise proposals simply did not go far enough to save his skin from the wrath of Palestinian Muslim militants.

Israeli officials believe that the Al-Aksa uprising was not the "spontaneous outburst" of popular anger that

Arafat maintained it was, but actually was preplanned by the Palestinian leader and his subordinates. They point to several bits of evidence to support this contention, including published remarks by Palestinian Minister for Jerusalem Affairs Faisal Husseini, who said nearly five months before the violence began that Palestinians would soon take to the streets if their demands regarding the holy city were not quickly met. They noted that Palestinian Authority–controlled media fully backed the "popular revolt" from the very beginning. Indeed, in the weeks before the new uprising broke out, Arafat's television stations had been repeatedly broadcasting graphic scenes of the original uprising of 1987–93 and of widespread riots that took place after the Israeli government opened a tourist tunnel along the base of the sacred Temple Mount in 1996. Palestinian participants in those actions were hailed as valiant heroes and martyrs whose "courageous acts of resistance" should be widely emulated today.

Many Israeli analysts believe that Arafat had no choice but to promote the latest explosion of violence, or at least to do very little to stop it, since the alternative was a Muslim-led revolt against his own administration. They said his repeated pledges that the Palestinian national flag would be hoisted in the near future over the stone walls, churches, and mosques of Jerusalem's Old City had been widely believed by most of his people, who would therefore never settle for a compromise peace deal that delivered anything less. Presuming that Barak could have sold the controversial Camp David proposals to the Israeli public—which is not at all certain—Clinton's plan probably would have resulted in the Palestinian flag flying high over most of the walls and holy sites of Jerusalem's historic Old City, but not over all of them. Anything less than everything would not have been enough for Palestinian Muslim militants, said the analyts, who would have aggressively opposed Arafat's perceived "surrender."

In my 1991 book, *Holy War for the Promised Land*, I was one of the first Western journalists to focus a spotlight on the Islamic Hamas movement, formed in 1988. I recall being criticized by some of my Jerusalem-based colleagues for doing so. They maintained that the extremist Islamic group would never amount to much and therefore didn't deserve the written attention I was giving it. Having studied the Muslim religion for over a decade and being a person of faith myself, albeit an evangelical Christian, I was fairly certain that Hamas and its sister movement, Islamic Jihad, would in fact assume an increasingly important role in Palestinian opposition to Israel. After Yasser Arafat signed the 1993 Oslo accord, the Islamic groups quickly became the main address for continuing Palestinian opposition to Israel's despised existence in the mainly Muslim Middle East. With the outbreak of the Al-Aksa "holy war," I am more convinced than ever before that unless Israel disappears from the map, Hamas, Islamic Jihad, and the Hizbullah militia in southern Lebanon will stay firmly planted in the very receptive regional soil, acting as a piercing thorn in the side of any future Israeli-Palestinian peace accord.

ZECHARIAH

The fact that the long-simmering Jerusalem issue has now clearly risen to the top of the bitter Arab-Israeli conflict should act as a warning that the prophesied end of days is fast approaching. The Bible makes abundantly clear, especially in the Old Testament Book of Zechariah, that the city will be at the center of history's final military conflict. Therefore, the fact that a hot verbal battle over Jerusalem has been raging for the past few decades, interspersed with two actual wars fought in parts of the city, should be enough of an alarm bell to alert Christians everywhere that the incendiary issue is in the ascendancy.

Zechariah's prophetic book is the largest of the so-called Minor Prophets. Martin Luther was among those who highly esteemed the fourteen-chapter book, calling it the "quintessence of the prophets." It contains many Hebraic prophetic elements found elsewhere in the Bible. The apocalyptic Revelation, recorded by the apostle John on the Greek island of Patmos, evinces several allusions to the book.

Unlike some of the ancient Jewish seers, little is known about Zechariah's life. His short genealogy in chapter 1, however, lists him as the grandson of Iddo, who is mentioned in the Book of Ezra as one of the returnees from the Babylonian captivity. This makes Zechariah one of the last of Israel's prophets before the Messiah's first advent. Iddo was evidently a temple priest, meaning Zechariah probably fulfilled the same family role. But his main accomplishment was to prophesy to the returning exiles, encouraging them to rebuild the destroyed temple, along with the Jewish capital city.

Zechariah, whose Hebrew name means "Yahweh remembers," records a series of angelically guided visions in chapters 1 through 6. They speak of golden lampstands, olive trees, flying scrolls, and chariots led by multicolored horses. From chapter 8 on, the prophet drops most of his symbolism and speaks almost exclusively of Jerusalem, Judah, and neighboring countries. This concentration on the holy city is why many have dubbed Zechariah "the prophet of Jerusalem."

Some Bible scholars insist that someone else authored the second half of the book after Zechariah's death. But conservative scholars mostly dispute this, saying the change of style and tone should not lead to the conclusion that oracles from two different sources have been combined in the book.

The focus on Jerusalem actually begins in chapter 2, where an angel proclaims that the city "will be inhabited without walls, because of the multitude of men and cattle within it" (v. 4). Then the Lord is quoted as warning that anyone who messes with Zion is touching "the apple of His eye" (v. 8). The Lord will one day dwell in the midst of the holy city, says verse 10. This will coincide with the inclusion of non-Jews in the saved people of God: "And many nations will join themselves to the LORD in that day and will become My people" (v. 11). Of course, this Gentile inclusion began in the time of Yeshua. But verse 11 will have its most complete fulfillment when Messiah returns to reign as King in Jerusalem.

In chapter 8, the Lord proclaims through Zechariah that He is "exceedingly jealous for Zion, yes, with great wrath I am jealous for her" (v. 2). The mention of "wrath" is the second hint that those who oppose God's plans and purposes for His chosen city and its people are opening themselves up for divine retribution. The rest of the chapter seems to speak of the return from Babylon that was already well underway in Zechariah's time. Yet the prophecy also telescopes into the very last days of history, as did Ezekiel 36 and 37. Both prophets look forward to the final restoration of Jerusalem spoken of in Psalm 102, a city where the Lord reigns supreme in glory.

Verse 3 echoes Micah 4:1–2 in referring to the ultimate exaltation of Jerusalem's Temple Mount. It will be called "the holy mountain" after the Lord "returns to Zion" to "dwell in the midst of Jerusalem." The city itself will then be called "the City of Truth." The Lord proclaims through Zechariah that old men and women will mix with young boys and girls, who will gather together on the streets of restored Jerusalem (vv. 4–5).

All of this must have seemed like extreme pie in the sky to the small band of Jewish laborers who were struggling to rebuild the decimated capital in Zechariah's day. This is alluded to in verse 6, although the skeptics there seem to be people living in the time of the final restoration spoken of in verse 3: "'If it is too difficult in the sight of the remnant of this people in those days, will it also be too difficult in My sight?' declares the Lord of hosts." The Lord appears to be hinting that while the return from Babylon—only several hundred miles east of Jerusalem—was dramatic enough, it will be nothing compared to the final ingathering.

Who could have imagined in Zechariah's time that the second Jewish homecoming would follow a worldwide diaspora lasting nearly two thousand years, capped by the murderous Holocaust? Such a return seemed almost impossible to scattered and persecuted Jews over the long centuries of worldwide exile, as intimated in verse 6. Yet the Jewish ingathering and upbuilding of Zion is now an ongoing historical fact. Indeed, almost half of the Jews on earth today are now living back in the Lord's land, compared to a minuscule percentage a mere one hundred years ago.

The God of Israel promises to "save My people from the land of the east and the land of the west," says verse 7. Then the restored nation will serve the Lord alone: "And I will bring them back, and they will live in the midst of Jerusalem and they will be My people and I will be their God in truth and righteousness" (v. 8). The Lord goes on to encourage the "remnant" of His people to be strong, assuring them that they will be treated well and will sow their crops in peace (vv. 9–12).

Verse 13 echoes Ezekiel 36 in pointing out that the house of Judah and the house of Israel were "a curse" in their international dispersion (during both the first and second exiles), apparently because their expulsions and foreign wanderings brought disgrace to God's good name. But now He vows to make them "a blessing" to all peoples, as amplified in verse 23. At that time, "many peoples and mighty nations will come to seek the LORD of hosts in Jerusalem and to entreat the favor of the LORD" (v. 22). Gentiles will not only petition Israel's Messiah, but will actually seek out His physical Jewish cousins because they have "heard that God is with you" (v. 23).

Chapter 9 features the wonderful prophecy that the Jewish Messiah would enter the holy city endowed with salvation. As we know from other Scripture passages, He would come to offer Himself as a blood sacrifice—to fulfill the divine requirement for cleansing from sin. Since sacrificial death was His immediate goal, the humble and just Messiah would not enter Jerusalem in some gilded chariot but "on a donkey, even on a colt, the foal of a donkey" (v. 9). What a picture of meekness and love!

The next verse, which speaks about the banishment of war and the dawn of universal peace, will not be fulfilled until the Messiah's *second* appearance in Jerusalem—this time in evident power and glory:

> And I will cut off the chariot from Ephraim,
> And the horse from Jerusalem;
> And the bow of war will be cut off.
> And He will speak peace to the nations;
> And His dominion will be from sea to sea,
> And from the River to the ends of the earth.

In chapter 10, God speaks again about His intention to recover His people from foreign exile. The prophecy is evidently not about the return from Babylon in

Zechariah's day. It looks forward to the final ingathering, since it refers to a still future exile and restoration:

> I will whistle for them to gather them together,
> For I have redeemed them;
> And they will be as numerous as they were before.
> When I scatter them among the peoples,
> They will remember Me in far countries,
> And they with their children will live and come back
> verses 8–9

Divine judgments against surrounding nations are spelled out in chapters 9 and 12. Apart from the Greeks, all three of the peoples alluded to, Syrians, Lebanese, and the Philistines, were opponents of Israel and Judah in Zechariah's time. Recent history records that their modern equivalents (which might include the Palestinians, whose modern name is derived from the ancient Philistines) were also sworn enemies as the second ingathering was taking place over the past century. In fact, all participated in wars against the reborn Jewish state. I believe that all will also play an important role in Israel's next prophesied war, as I detail in chapter 5.

In Zechariah 12, God is preparing to reveal something very important about Israel and Jerusalem. Therefore, He prefaces His remarks by restating some of His unrivaled credentials: "Thus declares the LORD who stretches out the heavens, lays the foundation of the earth, and forms the spirit of man within him" (v. 1). In other words, this is no local deity about to speak; this is the all-knowing Creator of the universe.

Israel's eternal King declares that He is "going to make Jerusalem a cup that causes reeling *to all the peoples around;* and when the siege is against Jerusalem, it will also be against Judah" (v. 2, italics mine). So, God is going to make the peoples who surround Israel (which include the three mentioned above) drink out of the chalice of Jerusalem. This will apparently occur in the form of a military siege against both the city itself and the surrounding hills of Judea. But this action will cause the attackers to stagger backward as if they had drunk poison from a cup.

Some Bible scholars teach that this verse was fulfilled during the Roman siege against Judea and Jerusalem in A.D. 66–70. I strongly question that view since distant Rome was hardly a "surrounding" country. More than that, the powerful Roman legions did not stagger away from the battle, but incinerated the vanquished city. Since there is no other historical occurrence since Zechariah's time that even remotely matches this prophecy, I believe the verse is probably referring to a future, regional war aimed at retaking Jerusalem for Islam. In light of current events, I think this could well be Israel's next major conflict.

Verse 3 is often directly linked to the preceding one. I suspect, however, that the two verses are referring to separate battles over Jerusalem that occur in the same historic era—the prophesied end of days. The first war will involve Mideast forces only. The second, addressed in verse 3, will include troops from around the world. This is clearly stated in the second half of the verse: "And *all the nations of the earth* will be gathered against it" (italics mine). In this international war, fighting against Jerusalem doesn't just cause reeling. The holy city is likened to a "heavy stone" that "severely injures" all who lift it up.

I suspect that the darkening foreshadows of earth's final conflict, involving all the nations on the planet, can already be seen today in the violent Israeli-Palestinian dispute. From the very first moments of the Al-Aksa uprising, Yasser Arafat made plain that his most pressing political demand was for an "international protection force" to be immediately sent to the contested zones in order to "stop Israeli attacks upon my unarmed people." An Arab-led attempt to secure United Nations approval for such a force was only narrowly thwarted when the United States voted no in March 2001. However, Palestinian leaders vowed to continue pushing for an international force. The proposed force would obviously mean the gathering of soldiers from around the world to the very land the prophets foretold would host the final battle of history. Their mission would be to help resolve the violent Israeli-Palestinian conflict that has at its core the explosive issue of Jerusalem.

Other portions of Scripture fill in more details about the final world war. In the Book of Revelation, it is called Armageddon. Although that name comes from the ancient town of Meggido, located in the fertile Jezreel valley which stretches across northern Israel from Mount Carmel to the Jordan River basin, the war is obviously not an attempt to conquer the ruins of that town or the crop-filled sprawling valley. The final war will clearly be fought over the issue of Jerusalem and surrounding areas. The Jezreel valley is merely a fairly close, broad, flat, and sparsely populated staging area where military forces can be strategically organized for the ultimate assault on the city. It already hosts Israel's northernmost air force base, whose runways could easily be used by international aircraft in a future attack against Jerusalem.

Unlike many end-time prophecy buffs, I suspect that this final battle dovetails with the one described in Ezekiel 38 and 39. Known as Gog and Magog, it is popularly thought to precede the rise of the Antichrist world ruler. Therefore, it also comes well before Armageddon, which Revelation 16:16 says occurs at the end of Antichrist's rule. Others see the Ezekiel invasion as occurring after the Lord's millennial reign on earth. I will examine this topic more closely in chapter 10.

The best source of biblical information about the final worldwide attack on Jerusalem is found in Zechariah 14. Again the Lord reveals that He will "gather all the nations against Jerusalem to battle" (v. 2). Sadly, the verse then goes on to foretell that the city will be captured. This will result in houses being plundered and women raped. As if that is not bad enough, half of the city's besieged residents will be exiled. It is interesting to note that the modern city was divided in two from 1948 until 1967, and the Arab world demands that the eastern half, the part captured by Israeli forces in 1967, be handed back to them. Could the "half-city" exile spoken of here refer to a forced redivision of the city?

Wait a minute! What about God's earlier promise to "severely injure" those nations who come up against Jerusalem? It sounds like it is Israel that is mortally wounded here. Thankfully, Zechariah 12:4–9 quotes Israel's Savior as saying He plans to fully defend His chosen people during this final battle. According to Zechariah's prophecy, God will partially do so by supernaturally strengthening the inhabitants of Judah and Jerusalem so that they are enabled to fight back against their enemies and eventually prevail.

Verses 8 and 9 are especially clear about this: "In that day the LORD will defend the inhabitants of Jerusalem, and the one who is feeble among them in that day will be like David, and the house of David will be like God, like the angel of the LORD before them. And it will come about in that day that I will set about to destroy all the nations that come against Jerusalem."

So, the Lord Himself will intervene on behalf of His people in two ways: He will first strengthen them to fight on their own and afterwards take on the attacking nations Himself. He will apparently allow many Jerusalem residents to suffer and die in the process. But with God's help, the remnant of Israel will ultimately triumph.

But won't two-thirds of all Israelis perish in the last days' military struggle? This idea is commonly taught, based on Zechariah 13:8–9. The preceding verses, however, are apparently about the Lord's first coming and death on a cross, which later resulted in His persecuted flock being scattered from the land (vv. 6–7). Since that coincided with Jerusalem's destruction and the slaughter of a good part of Judea's Jewish citizens by Roman soldiers, many scholars believe verses 8 and 9 refer to that era and not to the end-time battles described in chapters 12 and 14. I agree with this interpretation, although many Jews will certainly be wounded or die in the predicted final siege against Jerusalem and Judea.

The Lord's intention to forcefully intervene after His holy city is captured is clearly revealed in 14:3: "Then the Lord will go forth and fight against those nations, as when He fights on a day of battle." While the concept of the almighty God of the universe actually doing battle against Jerusalem's modern enemies is considered an offensive relic of the Dark Ages by many "progressive" Christians, Scripture nonetheless records here that it will someday take place.

God's direct intervention is just the first bit of good news for the embattled Jewish people! Not only will the invisible God get involved in the fray from heaven, but verse 4 says the visible Messiah will fight on their behalf from Jerusalem's Mount of Olives. But what is He doing up there? The Book of Acts unfolds that part of the story. As the resurrected Lord was ascending into the sky from the Mount of Olives, attending angels announced to His astonished disciples that He would return one day to the *exact place* from which He was ascending, due east of the Temple Mount.

57

History's final war will be won when the glorious Lord appears in Jerusalem. The Mount of Olives will be split in two, says verse 4, providing a route for residents to escape into the eastern desert. As that is happening, "the LORD, my God, will come, and all the holy ones with Him" (v. 5). So the Messiah won't return alone; a heavenly army will accompany Him. Of course, this exactly matches the apostle John's glowing description of the Lord of Hosts returning to earth, with myriad saints trailing behind Him (Rev. 19:14).

Zechariah 12 has more good news for God's long-suffering Jewish people. Not only will the sovereign Lord supernaturally strengthen the residents of Jerusalem and Judea; He will also pour out a spirit of grace and supplication on them. This will cause the entire house of David to "look on Me *whom they have pierced;* and they will mourn for Him, as one mourns for an only son, and they will weep bitterly over Him like the bitter weeping over a first-born" (v. 10, italics mine). Why would the rescued Jewish people react like this? After all, they are finally seeing their awesome heavenly protector and defender. Shouldn't that cause great joy? Why the tears?

The answer is found in the phrase "look on Me whom they have pierced." Somehow, the inhabitants of Jerusalem have sorely wounded their divine defender. Zechariah doesn't elaborate, but the New Testament and history do. For the most part, the house of David rejected the one who rode into Jerusalem on a donkey bringing salvation to Zion. For centuries afterward, His name would be considered an unutterable curse, His memory a disgrace. Any Jew professing Yeshua as Lord would be excommunicated and considered as dead. All this would occur after the Messiah's flesh was torn by Roman nails in Jerusalem—literally fulfilling Isaiah's prophecy that the Man of Sorrows would be "pierced through for our transgressions" and "crushed for our iniquities" (53:5).

Zechariah foretells that after the chosen people "look on" their Redeemer King (which could be either externally, actually seeing Him descending toward the Mount of Olives, or internally), a period of intense mourning for this forsaken Son will follow. But it doesn't end there. A "fountain will be opened for the house of David and for the inhabitants of Jerusalem, for sin and for impurity" (13:1). This cleansing fountain—Messiah's sacrificial blood atonement offered in Jerusalem many centuries before—graciously adds spiritual salvation to the physical deliverance described in chapters 12 and 14. The people of Israel will be saved in both body and spirit. No better news is possible.

After the Messiah returns in glory to the Mount of Olives, "living waters shall flow out of Jerusalem" toward the western Mediterranean Sea, and also toward the eastern Dead Sea, which will be brought back to life (14:8). No more drought for this dry and thirsty land! We are told in Ezekiel 47:8 that these effervescent waters, cascading down the once-parched valleys of Judea from underneath the elevated Temple Mount, will make the world's salty sea waters fresh.

The final good news in Zechariah's remarkable book comes in chapter 14 verses 9, 11, and 16. There will be no more despots or evil regimes after the Lord returns, for He alone will be "king over all the earth" (v. 9).

Verse 11 is especially moving to me. I have filed a number of radio news reports detailing several deadly terror attacks in Jerusalem over the years. I also covered Saddam Hussein's threats to bomb the city with Scud missiles during the 1991 Gulf War. But when the Lord returns, "there will be no more curse, for Jerusalem will dwell in security" (v. 11). Praise the Lord!

After revealing more of the negative consequences that those nations who come up against Jerusalem will suffer, Zechariah ends with reference to a joyous biblical feast that I am privileged to celebrate every year here in the holy city: "Then it will come about that any who are left of all the nations that went against Jerusalem will go up from year to year to worship the King, the LORD of hosts and to celebrate the Feast of Booths" (v. 16). May such fantastic visits to the redeemed and thriving city of the great King be in all of our futures!

4

Judea and Samaria

===

I was pretty much a pacifist during my teen years. I shared the conviction of many American male peers that it was a waste of fleeting youth and time to fight for the southern half of divided Vietnam. I was shocked when my draft lottery number was picked in late 1973 (for younger readers, the U.S. military actually based the draft in those days on randomly chosen lotto balls numbered with all three hundred and sixty-five birth dates). My birthday's lucky draw was among the top fifty numbers, meaning I would probably be making a beeline across the Pacific unless I could follow my three older brothers (and millions of other American young men) in securing a student or medical deferment.

Our determination to avoid the draft for this debatable war was strengthened by my cousin Dan's harrowing experience. The oldest son of career officer Uncle George, Dan was promised a place in the U.S. Navy band since he played a mean jazz trumpet. But his father's military connections couldn't keep our relative out of the Southeast Asian conflict. Assigned to a PT boat on the dangerous Mekong River, he had little time to blow his horn. The entire Dolan clan was stunned in early 1968 when news reports revealed that nine out of ten PT boats patrolling the river had been sunk during the initial days of the Communist Tet offensive. We spent many unsettled hours hoping and praying for Dan, despite the odds, before finally learning with great relief that he was on the boat left afloat. Then we joined our countrymen in grieving for the families who were not so fortunate.

Living in Israel since 1980, my attitude toward the military has undergone a sea change. Here the conflicts are not distant ones that hardly threaten the homeland. In Israel the dangers are close by and understandable to all. There was significant internal dissent over the wisdom of Israel's only self-initiated war, the Lebanon conflict of 1982, which only grew over time. But apart from that, most battles have been forced upon the tiny Jewish state, Saddam Hussein's unprovoked Scuds being the last example. Additionally, the military draft here does not just spread its net over the hapless underclass, as it basically did in 1960s America. Almost every eighteen-year-old Jew, male and female, is called up for military service.

After it became apparent that the new Al-Aksa uprising was not just a flash in the pan, quite a few of my Israeli friends and acquaintances were called up for reserve duty. In previous years, many such part-time soldiers were sent to buttress regular forces in the hot battle zone of southern Lebanon, with a minority serving in Judea and Samaria (better known around the world as the West Bank) and the compact Gaza Strip south of Tel Aviv. The need for soldiers to patrol Arab towns and villages in the two disputed areas had diminished greatly after the 1993 Oslo accord was signed, with large chunks of them being transferred to full or partial Palestinian political and security control. However, with Israeli troops now entirely out of Lebanon (having withdrawn in May 1999), and with the Al-Aksa uprising centering on the contested territories and Jerusalem, many of my friends are once again doing their reserve military duty in the hallowed hills of Judea and Samaria and in the teeming Gaza Strip.

When traveling abroad, I am often asked questions concerning Israel's military capabilities and policies. I have examined these topics quite extensively in my previous book, *Israel at the Crossroads,* and therefore won't repeat that material here. I am also frequently asked about the Palestinians and about Israeli settlements in Judea and Samaria, the small biblical heartland territory that was annexed by Jordan in 1950 and renamed the West Bank of the Kingdom of Jordan. I examined the political aspects of these questions in my previous book. In this chapter, I look at several biblical prophecies related to them.

I will presume that you are a normal reader and are therefore absorbing this chapter after reading the preceding two, instead of the other way around (Israelis read from right to left, but then that's the way Hebrew letters are laid out). If so, you already realize that I view Israel's 1967 capture of Jerusalem's ancient Old City as sanctioned by God. This is not based on any private notions of the Lord's will nor on personal messages from on high.

Israel's end-time return to the earthly Zion is foretold in various Bible passages, as I have hopefully demonstrated. For the Jewish people, the heart of Jerusalem is, of course, the Old City's Temple Mount. But what land is central to the Palestinian Arabs? And what about Israel's 1967 conquest of other parts of Jordan's former West Bank? (I say "former," since the late King Hussein officially revoked any claim to the area in 1988, which rendered the modern name "West Bank" effectively null and void.) What does the Bible say, if anything, about these steamy issues?

As always, different people will respond in different ways. This is especially true when the questions concern such political hot potatoes as the ones mentioned above. Someone always seems unhappy whatever answer you give. So with that caveat in mind, I will now present in writing the gist of my usual oral responses.

The Bible lays down clear guidelines regarding Israel and its surrounding Gentile neighbors, which I believe are still applicable today, with a few possible modifications. I am also convinced that the Hebrew prophets foretold that the Jewish people would return to Israel's biblical heartland—known for millennia by the ancient names Judea and Samaria—in the last days of history and that God Himself would have a significant hand in that restoration.

Since that is a controversial position even among Bible-believing Christians, let alone among Palestinian supporters, one point is essential to make right away: The Bible unequivocally states that the Promised Land, like all of the earth, belongs to God and not to any one people or tribe. It also records, however, that He unilaterally chose to permanently cede His Promised Land deed to Abraham and his descendants forever (Gen. 17:8). Over the patriarch's protests, God clarifies that the title will not pass through Ishmael, but through Isaac

(17:21), and later through Jacob (28:13–15) and his twelve sons. Ishmael is hardly left out, however; he will become the father of twelve princes and a great nation (17:20).

If one accepts the Bible as authoritative, as many obviously do not, then the land ownership question is easily resolved. Nevertheless, the Bible records that the Jewish people were repeatedly warned that sustained residence in the land was dependent on their observance of God's laws. In fact, Moses foretold that they would be driven out of the land because of their sins, as they most certainly were. Yet he also revealed that they would ultimately be restored by God (Deut. 30:1–5). But as we saw in Ezekiel 36, the final Jewish return from well-deserved exile is a sovereign act of a covenant-keeping God, done mainly for the sake of His own reputation. It is therefore not contingent at all upon earlier or even contemporary Jewish behavior.

During the drawn-out return from Egypt, Joshua was told to conquer Canaan and thus implement God's land pact for the first time. In the process, his forces were to utterly wipe out the seven people groups then residing in the land, as commanded by God through Moses (Deut. 7:1–2, 5, 16). While considered extreme, if not genocidal to many modern readers, the Bible explains the reasons for such a wholesale slaughter. God wanted His Jewish people to be especially holy in order to play a pivotal role in His unique redemptive purposes for all of humanity (7:6). They would be seriously corrupted if they let their enemies live (7:3–4), since Canaan's pagan occupants were enslaved to all kinds of evil practices, including idol worship and child sacrifice.

But those particular instructions applied only to the initial Jewish conquest in Joshua's day. What about the return from Babylon and even more so the current ingathering? Prophecies in Jeremiah, Ezekiel, Daniel,

Zechariah, and other places make no mention of a divine order to exterminate the people who occupied the Lord's land during the Assyrian-Babylonian exile. Returning Jews did fight against harassment by their enemies (Ezra 4), but they mainly did this by referring to their legal right to return to their homeland, granted by Persian King Cyrus. Their opponents, who included a prominent Arab (Neh. 2:19), were told that they had "no portion, right, or memorial in Jerusalem" (2:20). Still, they were not driven out of the land or slaughtered en masse, not even after the restored Jewish state briefly became powerful once again.

Why was there one divine settlement policy in Joshua's time and another after the Babylonian return? A transformed moral climate seems to be the difference. Cyrus is actually called an anointed shepherd of God by the prophet Isaiah (44:28; 45:1). This is the same Isaiah who also reveals that Gentiles will one day seek the Lord in Jerusalem and be included in the Messiah's worldwide reign of peace (2:3; 42:1–4). Micah and others echo this. In response to Jonah's preaching, pagan residents of the great Assyrian capital of Nineveh actually repented in sackcloth and ashes, much to the prophet's chagrin. The Book of Daniel includes an extraordinary account of Babylonian King Nebuchadnezzar acknowledging Israel's God as the only true sovereign (4:34–35). His change of heart followed a wilderness experience of divine punishment (vv. 31–33).

So by the time of the first return, knowledge of Israel's moral God had already spread to Israel's Gentile neighbors, even though most were still living as pagans. Positive moral results from the Jewish people's ordained role to be a "light to the nations" were already being felt on earth as rulers and their citizens became aware of the justice, righteousness, and miracle-working power of the God worshiped in Jerusalem.

If that was the case during the time of the first return, it is thrice so today. Most of the current non-Jewish residents of the Lord's land are either Muslims or Christians. Both religions sprang up from Jewish roots. Both revere the Hebrew prophets and holy book, even though each religion maintains that it has superseded traditional Judaism.

Christianity was entirely Jewish in its seminal years. It is centered on a wise, compassionate, miracle-working Galilee rabbi named Yeshua, whom Christians believe to be *Israel's* promised Messiah, and on His twelve equally Jewish apostles. Major supporting roles are played by His Jewish mother (how can a Jewish momma be left out of the script?), mainly Jewish disciples, and later by an initially rabid rabbi named Saul.

While more divergent from historic Judaism in some important ways, Islamic doctrines are clearly founded on Judeo-Christian teachings and values. Muslim moral codes are heavily influenced by the Bible. There is no comparison between, for instance, accepted social and sexual norms of the ancient Canaanite inhabitants of the land and those of Islamic residents today. If anything, local Arab Muslims and Christians in the early twentieth century more faithfully reflected traditional biblical standards than the many agnostic Jewish immigrants who arrived from Russia and elsewhere.

In summary, it should be crystal clear that God did not order or intend for His returning Jewish people to wipe out Gentile inhabitants of the land. Indeed, the Bible makes clear that even in ancient times non-Jews would be allowed to live peacefully in the land and would actually be granted equal statutory and sacrificial religious rights if they agreed to be circumcised (Exod. 12:48–49) and gave homage to the God of Israel (Num. 9:14; 15:14–16). It is evident, however, that they had to recognize Jewish primacy in the land, in accor-

dance with the everlasting land covenant that God made with Abraham, Isaac, and Jacob.

Although physical circumcision is not a requirement for Gentiles wishing to serve on God's worship team today (Acts 15:19–20), there is no biblical reason to maintain that Gentile recognition of Jewish sovereignty in the land has ever been rescinded.

So how should Christians view Israel's 1967 conquest and occupation of Judea and Samaria, along with the Gaza Strip, Golan Heights, and Sinai Peninsula? Well, Sinai is obviously no longer an issue since it has been returned in its entirety to Egyptian control. In biblical terms, it is arguable whether the vast desert area was ever intended by God to be part of the Promised Land. Historically, it was never a Jewish settlement zone. Therefore, Menachem Begin faced only token religious opposition when he agreed to pull all of his forces out of the Sinai in 1978, dismantling a few Jewish settlements in the process.

The Gaza Strip seems to fit into some of the biblical descriptions of Israel's divinely sanctioned borders, as does the Golan Heights. Ironically, Gaza was never a center of Hebrew settlement in ancient times but did have a Jewish presence in the centuries before the second ingathering began in the late 1800s. The crowded narrow strip of land, nestled along the Mediterranean coast south of Tel Aviv, is certainly not central to Jewish religious life. The same can be said of the Golan plateau above Israel's northern Galilee panhandle, although there is ample archaeological evidence that Jewish life thrived in the fertile heights in biblical times.

JEREMIAH 32 AND 33

The hilly regions of Judea and Samaria are another matter altogether. The areas north and south of Jerusalem were indisputably Israel's ancient, hallowed heartland. It was in them that God instructed Abraham, "Lift up your eyes and look from the place where you are, northward and southward and eastward and westward; for all the land which you see, I will give it to you and to your descendants forever" (Gen. 13:14–15). It was there that Isaac and Jacob were born, and it was in the Judean town of Hebron where the patriarchs and all of their wives were buried, apart from Rachel, who was interred on her way to the Judean town of Bethlehem. King David hailed from Bethlehem, first reigned as king in Hebron, and then conquered the Jebusite "stronghold of Zion," Jerusalem.

The quaint little town was the very spot that God chose for His hallowed sanctuary to be built says 2 Chronicles 33:7: "In this house and in Jerusalem, which I have chosen from all the tribes of Israel, I will put My name forever." No other place on earth has such an exalted calling, and it is located in the northern part of Judea, which borders the hills and dales of Samaria. All of the kings of Israel and Judah established their thrones in the consecrated mountains. Almost all of the prophets performed their inspired tasks and are buried there. Finally, the most important events in all of history—the birth, death, and resurrection of the humble Lamb of God—took place in the waterless slopes of Judea.

Thus, establishing the overwhelming importance of Judea and Samaria to the Jewish people, and also to Christians, is an absurdly easy task. Clearly, the subdivided hilly region (a mere thirty odd miles wide from east to west and some eighty miles long from north to south) is the heart and soul of world Judaism. No Rome rivals it for Jewish religious affections. True, the ancient monotheistic religion is more about faith in one God and spiritual values than about bits and pieces of earth. But Judaism's land connection was designed by God, who not only promised specific territory to His covenant people, but also established several annual feasts that are intricately linked to the land.

I often speak about the time in 1996 when I was privileged to be a guest at the Jewish Community Center in Melbourne, Australia. It was during the annual Feast of Shavuot ("Weeks" in English, but better known to Christians as Pentecost). The public building was decorated with bundles of wheat and other fruits and grains in accordance with the biblical guidelines for celebrating the "first harvest" feast (Lev. 23:16–21). As I looked around the nicely decorated center, I couldn't help being both amused and amazed. No way is early June—when the feast was celebrated that year according to the Jewish calendar—the time of first harvest Down Under! It is the end of autumn in the Southern Hemisphere, when the nights are long and the fields lie mainly fallow, at least in the Melbourne area.

Why were intelligent, well-educated Australian Jews celebrating a first harvest feast just before the official onset of winter? Because that is what is done, per God's command, in the Promised Land! Following the same principle, observant Jews in Ireland pray for the "early rains" to begin each October—a thoroughly ridiculous petition on the boggy island—because that is what is done in the dry and thirsty land!

Napoleon is said to have passed by a synagogue that could not contain the passionate sounds of weeping and moaning inside. When he asked what the fuss was all about, he was informed that penitent Jews were simply conducting their traditional prayer service for the restoration of the Jewish temple in Jerusalem. The great French emperor reportedly replied that any people who get so worked up over an ancient, destroyed religious center will surely have their prayers fulfilled one day.

Just as Napoleon predicted, the Jewish people are now the sovereign landlords once again in their beloved holy city, even though that status is disputed by the nations. The Palestinians, backed by Muslim states and individuals around the world, want the walled Old City back. Gaining control will help them reiterate Islam's fifteen-hundred-year-old claim that it is the absolute and supreme revelation of spiritual truth. This is an extremely important goal to many Muslims who are concerned that such assertions have been severely tarnished by the modern Jewish conquest of Jerusalem.

So the holy city, and particularly the Temple Mount, is undoubtedly the most contested piece of real estate in the world today. Unlike the conflicting claims over Taiwan, Tibet, the northern islands of Japan, the border area between Pakistan and India, the Basque region of Spain, Kurdish portions of Turkey, and so on, the acrimonious dispute over Jerusalem is of direct religious significance to over half the people on earth.

But what about Judea and Samaria? Even if there is an enduring Jewish connection to the entire Promised

Land and not just to Jerusalem, should returning Jews be living in those mainly Arab areas? Does the Bible have anything specific to say on that question?

As I stated earlier in this chapter, I believe the Scriptures unequivocally reveal God's intention to restore his chosen people to both halves of Jordan's former West Bank. The authoritative prophet on this matter is the reluctant one, Jeremiah. He made most of his pronouncements in the stupefying days just before the Babylonian exile, when no one wanted to hear his warnings of pending doom and gloom. "Everything is gonna be all right, so shut up already!" is a colloquial summary of the responses he received. Despite the rebuffs, Jeremiah persisted to warn of the exile looming just ahead. His words, as we know now, were right on the mark.

Jeremiah's ominous messages did have some bright spots, however. Like all the prophets, God used him to reveal good things for the future as well. Specifically, the scattered Jewish people would return from exile and reinhabit their decimated cities and towns. They would even be the recipients of a new covenant, one that would actually place God's law directly inside their hearts (31:31–33).

Many of Jeremiah's restoration prophecies seem to address both the first and final returns. Thus, in 23:5, God is quoted as alluding to the promises first recorded in Isaiah 11. Both passages foretell that a "righteous Branch of David" will be raised up to reign as king over Israel. Judah will then "be saved and . . . dwell securely" (v. 6). Indeed, the regathering "from all the countries where I had driven them" (v. 8) ends with Messiah's righteous rule. It will be so magnificent that the exodus from Egypt—the heart of the Jewish Passover liturgy— will no longer be verbally recalled (v. 7). The recovery from Babylon was not that stupendous, next to nothing compared to the grand exodus from Egypt that featured parting seas and a burning bush. But the ultimate restoration will sparkle with even greater glory than the desert journey, since the returning King of Glory will finally be seated on His majestic Jerusalem throne!

Jeremiah's restoration revelations reach their climax in chapters 30 through 33. They begin with God's pledge to "restore the fortunes of My people Israel and Judah," clarifying that He is talking about their physical return to "the land that I gave to their forefathers" (30:3). Then there is a brief reference to a time of tremendous distress for Jacob's offspring, often referred to as Jacob's Trouble. Some interpret this as the Holocaust, while others see it as a still future period of upheaval during the Antichrist's brief but brutal reign (more on this in chapter 10). Despite the brief reference to great distress, returning Jews are promised that they will be "quiet and at ease" in their land (v. 10). Ominously, God says He will "destroy completely" all the countries where His people had been scattered (v. 11). However, other passages reveal that unnamed "sheep" nations will not be entirely wiped out in the final judgment, while other "goat" nations will be annihilated.

The first mention of Israel's hilly heartland is found in Jeremiah 31:5–6. It comes right after God speaks tenderly about His chosen people, saying, "I have loved you with an everlasting love; therefore I have drawn you with lovingkindness" (v. 3). This is one of many verses that balance out God's sterner remonstrations against His exiled people, such as the "reputation clearing" ones I quoted from Ezekiel 36. Yes, He will bring them back to the land in order to erase the shame that their worldwide wandering brought to His own good name. But He will also restore His wayward children because He deeply loves them. Do they deserve that love? No more than they deserve to be drawn back to the Promised

Land. But our God is, thankfully, a covenant-keeping redeemer. That is good news for Jew and Gentile alike.

The rebuilt "virgin of Israel" will "again . . . plant vineyards on the hills of Samaria" (Jer. 31:4–5). More than this, a day will come when "watchmen on the hills of Ephraim shall call out, 'Arise, and let us go up to Zion, to the LORD our God'" (v. 6). This seems to be referring to a time when God's presence in Jerusalem will again be manifest in a very tangible way. Such was not the case after the Babylonian exile, when the *Shekinah* glory did not return to the rebuilt temple. But it will follow the second ingathering when the Messiah Himself—the visible image of the invisible God—sits on His throne ruling the world from Jerusalem.

More evidence that Jeremiah's prophecy refers mainly to the final ingathering is contained in 31:8, where God says He is bringing His people back "from the remote parts of the earth." While this was clearly not the case in the Babylonian return, it is obviously true in our day. Immigrants have moved to Israel from Australia, New Zealand, Hawaii, California, Argentina, and other places on the opposite side of the globe.

After speaking of the coming new covenant, God reveals that His chosen people will only cease to be a nation before Him if the "fixed order of the moon and the stars" is altered, and if the "heavens above can be measured" (31:35–37). Guess which world power has attempted to measure the universe, only to find it immeasurable. A quick read of these verses might have saved us American taxpayers some money, although NASA's Explorer satellite program has produced some intriguing news reports.

I often tell my audiences about the time in July 1991 when I visited friends on the big island of Hawaii. My arrival coincided with a total eclipse of the sun, best seen, said the astronomers, on the isolated Pacific island chain. It was the most spectacular show on earth! I marveled at how the dark face of the moon, with a circumference of only some 6,800 miles, appeared to perfectly cover the glowing face of the sun, even though the latter has a diameter about four hundred times greater! How come they appeared to be exactly the same size to the naked eye during the eclipse, affording a breathtaking view of towering solar flares? It is, of course, due to their celestial locations in relation to the earth. The begging question is, Who or what placed them in such orbits to give us earthlings this periodic heavenly thriller? The usual scientific answer is random chance. The biblical answer is an intelligent, creative, and powerful God, the same God who said that Israel would remain a distinct nation unless this "fixed order" is altered.

Chapter 32 of Jeremiah begins with the prophet being jailed by King Zedekiah. This takes place as the Babylonians besiege Jerusalem. Despite his imprisonment, Jeremiah buys a field north of the city as a sign that "houses and fields and vineyards shall again be bought in this land" after the pending exile is over (v. 15).

This theme is expanded upon toward the end of the chapter, beginning in verse 37. Here, however, the weeping prophet seems to telescope once more into the far-off distant future, describing things that did not take place after the Babylonian return.

God declares that he will gather His people "out of all the lands to which I have driven them in My anger, in My wrath, and in great indignation; and I will bring them back to *this place* and make them dwell in safety" (v. 37, italics mine). Notice that the Lord is not going to restore them to any other spot on earth, but only to their sanctified land. After this task is accomplished, they "shall be My people, and I will be their God; and I will give them one heart and one way, that they may fear Me always, for their own good and for the good of their children after them" (vv. 38–39).

Many scholars believe this prophecy was fulfilled when the Messiah shed his blood on Golgotha for Israel's sins and for the sins of the world. As noted earlier, however, a majority of Jews living in the land at the time of Christ rejected God's gracious, preannounced gift. Indeed, this prophecy will only become reality for most Jewish Israelis when the Lord comes a second time to defend Jerusalem, as we saw in Zechariah 12.

The new covenant in Messiah's blood is elaborated on in verses 40 and 41. But again, a complete fulfillment of these promises seems to still lie ahead: "And I will make an everlasting covenant with them that I will not turn away from them, to do them good; and I will put the fear of Me in their hearts so that they will not turn away from Me. And I will rejoice over them to do them good, and I will *faithfully plant them in this land* with all My heart and with all My soul" (italics mine).

The inherent implication here is that the restored Jewish remnant will not be uprooted any more from their land. If God's promise was only meant for the returning exiles from Babylon, He miserably failed to keep His word. The Jews remained at home for just over six hundred years, and that partially under foreign, pagan rule, before the Romans flung them out of the Promised Land.

How is it possible that the Great Gardener would "faithfully plant" His Jewish children in their native soil and not be able to keep them there? He will do so, says Jeremiah 32:42, but only after the second ingathering. A long exile, much worse than the Assyrian-Babylonian one, lay ahead. It would feature unparalleled disasters for the dispersed Jewish people, including violent expulsions from many countries, accusations that they caused Europe's monstrous Black Death, the bloody Spanish Inquisition, deadly pogroms in Russia and elsewhere, and the unspeakable Holocaust. Yet God would eventually save His beloved people and fulfill every good word to them: "For thus says the LORD, 'Just as I brought all this great disaster on this people, so I am going to bring on them all the good that I am promising them'" (v. 42).

What will fulfillment of God's good promises entail? In verses 43 and 44, it involves the literal buying back of fields made desolate by the invading Chaldeans. While the mention of the Chaldeans—another name for the Babylonians—seems to place these verses firmly at the time of the first ingathering, the rest of the context, as I have hopefully shown, is largely about the future final return. The word "Chaldeans" here may only be a catchall term for non-Jewish powers that would host dispersed Jews. Therefore, I believe verse 44, which details the *exact* parts of the Promised Land God would restore to Jewish control, applies to our time as well.

Six particular areas are named in verse 44. They are the land of Benjamin, just north of Jerusalem; the environs of the city, which implicitly includes Jerusalem itself; the cities of Judah, or Judea; the cities of the "hill country," another name for Samaria; the cities of the lowland, or the flat coastal plane; and the cities of the south, or the Negev desert. It is interesting to note that the 1947 United Nations partition plan only allowed for Jewish resettlement in a part of Jerusalem (but not under Israeli sovereignty), along the coastal plane, and in the sparsely populated Negev. Existing Jewish communities south of Bethlehem, near Hebron, and in the hills of Samaria would presumably be uprooted, as actually occurred during the 1948 war.

Israel's War of Independence secured Jewish control over half of Jerusalem but not over most of its environs. The land of Benjamin, the cities of Judah, and the entire hill country of Samaria fell under Jordanian control. However, Israeli forces captured all of these areas in the June 1967 war. Since then, over 250,000 Jews have settled in portions of eastern Jerusalem and in over 130 communities in the former West Bank.

Was God behind the 1967 Israeli conquests? While it may be politically correct to say no, it seems likely from these Scriptures and others that the answer is yes. This response is strengthened by chapter 33, which starts out with God reaffirming His promise to "restore the fortunes of Judah and the fortunes of Israel" (v. 7). Again, this was partially fulfilled after the Babylonian return. But in verse 13, the same six areas are listed once more, but in a shuffled order. The list begins with Samaria and ends with the land of Judah. The fact that God, speaking through Jeremiah, *twice* detailed the exact portions of the land to be resettled by returning Jews appears to be quite significant to me. The Lord really wants us to know that these *specific areas* were what He meant when he pledged in 32:41 to restore His people to "this land."

Further proof that verse 13 speaks of an end-time restoration is contained in verses 14 through 16. The return will coincide with the rule of the righteous Branch of David, who is first mentioned by Isaiah. This is not referring to Yeshua's first advent, but His glorious reign from Jerusalem, when "He shall execute justice and righteousness on the earth" (33:15). At that time, "Judah shall be saved and Jerusalem shall dwell in safety, and this is the name by which she shall be called: the LORD is our righteousness" (v. 16). In other words, Jews will return to dwell in Judea and Samaria in the same time frame that Israel will experience her long-foretold spiritual and physical salvation. At that time, Jerusalem will not only dwell in complete safety—which was certainly not fulfilled after the first ingathering—but will receive a name change to *Yahweh Tzidkeinu.*

The biblical evidence I have presented in this chapter incontrovertibly demonstrates that God is behind the Jewish return to Israel's ancient biblical heartland. Yet even if this is true, it does not mean that Palestinian Arabs cannot also live in the land, as I noted earlier. They might even establish an autonomous state there, as the Oslo accords implied. However, if the Palestinians attempt to harm or dislodge resident Jews in the process, as has most certainly occurred on many occasions, they may find themselves acting against the revealed restoration work of Israel's God and thus against their own best spiritual and material interests.

Of course, the fact that God seems to clearly have a hand in the Jewish return to Israel's biblical heartland does not necessarily mean that he sanctioned every single community that has sprung up in the disputed zones. Maybe some have been located in an unnecessarily provocative position or manner, as most Palestinians and even some Israelis maintain. Certainly some Jewish residents have been extreme in their actions. Baruch Goldstein, a distraught doctor who shot dead more than two dozen Palestinians in Hebron's Tomb of the Patriarchs in 1994, was not acting under the influence of Israel's God, who forbids murder for any reason. But the overall biblical right of Jews to return to the hills of Judea and Samaria cannot be erased by individual actions, however evil or misguided they might be, nor by settlement efforts that may have taken place in an unwise or illegal manner.

The ancient prophecies we have examined indicate that the Lord overruled the 1947 UN partition plan and the 1948 Jordanian conquest and returned His remnant

Jewish people to their cherished biblical heartland. If so, all should beware of attempts to redivide the Lord's special land. For as the prophet Joel warns, this is one of the reasons that God will ultimately judge the nations in the "valley of Jehoshaphat" (3:2).

5

Israel's Next War

===

Saddam Hussein's Scud missile attacks were not nice. Like everyone in Israel, I donned a government-issued gas mask and sat night after night in my antichemical sealed room. It had been nearly a quarter century since an Arab military assault had focused on civilian areas. In 1967 the holy city of Jerusalem took the brunt of enemy fire. In 1991 chic and sassy Tel Aviv was hit, a city that had been spared from direct attack ever since Egyptian planes bombed it at the start of the 1948 war.

Israeli military analysts say that the 1991 Iraqi long-range missile strikes on the congested coastal plane were probably a foretaste of Israel's next major war. That war will not be fought on some remote battlefield like the Sinai desert or the sparsely populated Golan Heights by soldiers backed by tank and artillery fire and supported by air force jets and helicopter gunships. The next big bust-up, which seemed to be on its way after the new Palestinian uprising broke out in September 2000, will undoubtedly feature ballistic missile attacks on urban centers. Most chillingly, missile warheads are likely to contain chemical weapons and could in time even carry nuclear ones.

Israeli military planners, at the request of the government, have drawn up several scenarios as to how Israel's next war might begin and who might be involved. Although the projections are supposed to be top-secret, the Israeli and foreign press have published some details.

The speculative forecasts do not foresee an end to the danger of regional military confrontations if a final peace accord is signed between Israel and the Palestinians or between Israel and Syria. The Byzantine Middle East—swirling with ancient religious passions in countries run mostly by dictators and always full of labyrinthine intrigues—is simply too volatile to ever put away the guns for good. Peace pacts are merely pieces of paper that may or may not be honored over time. Despite having signed the preliminary Oslo accord with Yasser Arafat and then a peace agreement with Jordan, the late Yitzhak Rabin warned that one hundred years of violence and hatred could not possibly be overcome by the mere stroke of a pen. So the military planners continue to do their job while the politicians and diplomats do theirs.

Most war scenarios are said to start with a complete breakdown of the slow-moving Arab-Israeli peace process followed by local and then regional violence. The spark is usually an unresolved struggle over who gets what in Jerusalem. Indeed, this was the issue that set off the new Al-Aksa Palestinian uprising. Other con-

tentious issues, such as the fate of millions of Palestinian refugees and the future of Jewish settlements in
Judea and Samaria, could also be the flashpoint, or it
could be a combination of several issues. A major political assassination, a massive terror attack, or an armed
struggle for governmental control in Syria, Jordan,
Egypt, or Iraq might also ignite widespread violence,
say the scenarios.

The military postulations mainly project hostilities
breaking out either in Palestinian civilian centers or in
Lebanon, although missile attacks could also come out
of the blue from Syria, Iraq, or Iran. Even if major skirmishes broke out in Lebanon—a constant possibility
given its flammable mixture of Maronite Catholics, Shi-
ite and Sunni Muslims, and Palestinian refugees—or
missiles were launched from neighboring countries, the
projections warn that fighting could quickly spread to
Palestinian areas. If unrest began in Palestinian territory (as now seems the most obvious possibility, since
it has been ongoing since the last quarter of the year
2000), local Arab leaders might call upon their Mideast
Arab and Muslim brethren to back them up, thus setting off a regional war. Yasser Arafat essentially did that
during an emergency Arab League summit meeting in
October 2000 and at an international Islamic parley in
November.

Long before the new uprising began, I was regularly
asked during my frequent globetrottings about the
prospects for another major Mideast war, when and how
it could begin, and who might be involved. Often I've
been asked if the Bible has anything to say about this
topic. I believe it does.

When I moved to Israel in 1980, many Christians here
and abroad were expecting an imminent Soviet invasion. The superpower "detente" worked out between
Richard Nixon and Leonid Brezhnev in the early 1970s

was falling apart under the weight of the Kremlin's armed intervention in Afghanistan. Nuclear weapons were being manufactured like hotcakes on both sides of the East-West divide. Mutual Assured Destruction (MAD) was the strategic doctrine that both superpowers were clinging to in hopes that it would deter the other from firing the first round.

Amid the understandable hysteria of those days, authors Zola Levitt and Tom McCall came out with a fascinating book called *The Coming Russian Invasion of Israel*. The 1974 bestseller, featuring a forward by Hal Lindsey, was reprinted many times. Appearing in stores shortly after the Soviet-sponsored Yom Kippur War had exposed Israel's military vulnerability—rudely ending the period of heady euphoria that followed the 1967 triumph—the book hit a raw nerve. It was one of the first prophecy books I ever purchased, and a newer copy sits on my shelf to this day.

The authors wrote in their introduction, "The coming Russian invasion of Israel is not far off, and it will profoundly affect us all." More than a quarter century has passed since that bold statement was penned. In the intervening years, the sprawling Soviet empire has crumbled, and financially strapped Moscow has struggled to keep rebellious parts of its remnant Russian republic, like Chechnya and Dagestan, in line.

Yet for all that, I still agree with Zola Levitt (who has hosted me on his television program many times) and Tom McCall that a future Russian assault on Israel seems to be forecast in Ezekiel 38–39. I do not dispraise them for making many readers aware of the prophet's important Gog and Magog oracle. However, the foreword notes in their book, and not a few others like it, should serve as a warning that we cannot precisely know for sure how or when ancient biblical prophecies will be fleshed out on history's pages.

I have felt for many years that the next major attack on Israel will in fact not emanate from Russia. Instead, I believe it will be of more localized origin and lack superpower backing. I am not just saying this because the sprawling Soviet empire fell to pieces in the late 1980s and early 1990s. I adopted this position around 1983 when the Soviet bear was still big and boisterous. My revised stand was based on biblical research, coupled with new insights I gained from living in Israel and covering the 1982 war in Lebanon. These led me to conclude that the Gog and Magog invasion is most likely connected to the final war of Armageddon. I examine this issue more fully in chapter 10.

It seems likely to me that the outline for Israel's next major war is found in the ancient Hebrew Scriptures. Indeed, I suspect it is located in a psalm. Although we are not accustomed to thinking of the inspiring poems, prayers, and imagery as predictive in nature, we know from New Testament references that several psalms fit that bill. I have already written about Psalm 102 containing prophecies of Jerusalem's final restoration and events surrounding it. Psalm 22 speaks of Yeshua's crucifixion, including the detail that His garments would be divided up by His executioners (v. 18). Psalm 110 foretold that the Messiah would sit at the right hand of the Father (v. 1), hold the office of a priest (v. 4), and rule as king (v. 2).

I firmly believe that Psalm 83 also fits this prophetic category. It is one of a number of psalms attributed to Asaph, who was appointed by King David to be a worship leader in the Lord's anointed tabernacle (1 Chron. 6:31–33, 39). Asaph's sons were commissioned by David to "prophesy with lyres, harps, and cymbals" (1 Chron. 25:1) while Asaph himself "prophesied under the direction of the king" (v. 2). Therefore, we can legitimately

85

say that Asaph should be counted among Israel's ancient prophets.

Of course, biblical prophecy is as much *forthtelling* as it is foretelling. Asaph's main task was surely to proclaim the praises of God. However, while extolling Adonai's awesome virtues and attributes under King David's guiding hand, Asaph may well have also spoken predictively at times, as David himself did in Psalm 110.

PSALM 83

Psalm 83 is hardly poetic praise. Like Psalm 102, it is a heartfelt cry to God for deliverance from the psalmist's violent enemies. Unlike Psalm 102, however, Asaph clearly identifies his foes after revealing that they are hatching a malignant plot against the people of Israel. Let's take a detailed look.

The opening verse of Psalm 83 is identical in tone to that of Psalm 102, where the author begged God to "hear my prayer, . . . and let my cry for help come to Thee." Here Asaph pleads for God to "not remain quiet; do not be silent and, O God, do not be still." The reason for his distress is quickly revealed in verses 2–4:

> For behold, Thine enemies make an uproar;
> And those who hate Thee have exalted themselves.
> They make shrewd plans against Thy people,
> And conspire together against Thy treasured ones.
> They have said, "Come, and let us wipe them out as a
>   nation,
> That the name of Israel be remembered no more."

So Asaph's distress is caused by a military plot to destroy Israel. Notice that it is not a happenstance plan, but a considered conspiracy. Israel's enemies are said to be deliberately scheming together, drawing up shrewd plans to destroy the Jewish state. This is amplified in verse 5: "For they have conspired together with one mind; against Thee do they make a covenant." This orchestrated threat against Israel is ultimately directed at the Keeper of Israel. That could mean that their annihilation plot, if successful, would bring disgrace to the Lord's holy name, which He has chosen to link perpetually to the nation of Israel.

Who are these crafty enemies plotting to destroy the Jewish state? Asaph carefully lists them in verses 6 through 8:

> The tents of Edom and the Ishmaelites;
> Moab, and the Hagrites;
> Gebel, and Ammon, and Amalek;
> Philistia with the inhabitants of Tyre;
> Assyria also has joined with them;
> They have become a help to the children of Lot.

Those people groups were all enemies of ancient Israel. Various conflicts with one or the other are described in the Bible. While most were localized skirmishes, the battles with powerful Assyria spelled the end of the northern kingdom of Israel, as we examined earlier.

What is most intriguing to me is that Bible scholars say there is absolutely no evidence that such a far-reaching regional conspiracy—uniting ten enemies to the north, east, west, and southeast of Israel—ever occurred in ancient times! I quote from page 503 of the respected *Revised New Bible Commentary* (Grand Rapids: Eerdmans, 1970): "No such widespread alliance of adjacent states as is described in verses 6–8 is mentioned in the Old Testament." The commentary goes on to suggest that the named conspiracy may be the psalmist's "vivid way" of describing the "basic spiritual situation" of "secular opposition to the kingdom of God."

The textual evidence is strong that the psalmist is describing a tangible military alliance against Israel. This is not only confirmed by the plotters' shared intention to "wipe Israel out as a nation," but by the allusions to other historic battles later in the psalm. An actual military plan of attack is being described here, not just a spiritual assault on the kingdom of God. Indeed, such an alliance is so massive and intimidating that it surely would have been mentioned elsewhere in the Bible if it had been hatched in ancient times. That it was not mentioned is no reason to spiritualize the psalmist's words.

There are two other possibilities to consider. One is that the conspiracy was thwarted before it could get off the ground. This seems unlikely in that the listed enemies are said to have made "an uproar" (v. 2). We should have some biblical record if such a threatening united voice was ever raised against Israel.

The second possibility is the one I prefer: The psalmist was foreseeing a distant end-time plot against the restored Jewish state of Israel. It is quite interesting to note that modern descendants of all of the listed conspirators took part in the 1948 and 1967 preplanned—and shrilly trumpeted—assaults upon Israel. Is this just a coincidence? I suspect not.

Before we go any further, let's examine more closely who the ten listed people groups were and who their modern descendants probably are today.

The first seven peoples were all located east of Israel. They were seminomadic groupings whose fluid boundaries often overlapped. The first two, Edom and the Ishmaelites, have also become synonymous today with the entire Arab-Muslim world. This is because both peoples are thought to have migrated farther south into the Arabian Peninsula, the seat of Islam. On top of that, Ishmael is an important figure in Islamic theology. So in modern terms, these names could be referring to the oil-rich country of Saudi Arabia, which backed front-line Arab forces in 1948 and 1967, or to the entire Arab-Muslim world that stretches from Morocco to Oman. I believe the former option is the most probable one.

Moab was situated due east of the Dead Sea, with Edom to its south and Ammon to its north. The other listed eastern tribes, the Hagrites, Gebal, and Amalek, mingled in this area. Of course, the name Ammon is very much still with us today. Although usually spelled slightly differently from its biblical version, "Amman" is the capital of the modern kingdom of Jordan. The fledgling country where these ancient tribes roamed played a pivotal role in both the 1948 and 1967 wars.

Philistia and Tyre were Mediterranean seafaring powers in biblical days. Much is written about the battles King David had with the Philistines, who lived mainly along the coastal plain. The modern south Lebanese town of Tyre, which I visited several times after the 1982 Lebanon war, is located next to the ruins of the wealthy Phoenician port city. An ancient alliance between these two formidable powers and the seven eastern nations and the Philistines would have been quite threatening in Asaph's time.

It is not hard to identify the modern equivalent of Tyre. In biblical days, it was the leading city of Phoenicia. As noted above, the area is now part of the battle-scarred country of Lebanon. Israel's northern Arab neighbor officially took part in both the 1948 and 1967 wars, although its military contribution was negligible. Since 1970, South Lebanon has been the most active battle zone between Arab Muslims and Israeli Jews.

Historians believe that the Philistines sailed to Canaan from either the Greek island of Crete or from the Anatolian region of western Turkey. Wherever they originated, iron-wielding Philistine warriors proved formidable enemies to the settling Hebrew tribes. They were eventually absorbed by attacking Assyrian forces and disappeared as a separate people group.

Despite this, the name "Philistine" was resurrected by the Romans, who applied it to the Holy Land in an attempt to obliterate the Jewish connection to Zion. This took place after Roman legions destroyed Judea in A.D. 70. Rome also may have chosen the name because it belonged to an invading nation that was originally located to the west of Canaan, as was the case with Caesar's empire. Thus, as sea-going Philistines applied their name to Canaan's coastal plain, so the Romans would reapply the same name a thousand years later to decimated Judea.

One of the main Philistine towns was called Gaza. The modern city by that name has served as the unofficial seat of the Palestinian autonomy government since 1994, while the Gaza Strip is home to over one million Palestinians. This provides a strong hint as to who the modern equivalent of the ancient Philistines might be. An even greater clue is the very name "Palestinians," derived from the ancient Philistines. Local Arabs began to refer to themselves as Palestinians only after the collapse of the Ottoman empire at the end of World War I, when they desired to establish a separate political identity from surrounding Arab states. Nonetheless, they are now universally known by the ancient maritime name.

Although Palestinian Arabs were not a significant military power in either 1948 or 1967, they were at the political center of the wars that broke out in those years. Had their leaders wholeheartedly accepted the 1947 United Nations partition plan, as several prominent Palestinians recommended, surrounding Arab states would have found it morally difficult to attack the emerging Jewish state. Palestinian sufferings over the years have provided a potent excuse for the enduring "holy war" struggle against reborn Israel.

The last name mentioned in Psalm 83 belongs to the mighty Assyrian empire, which acts as "a help to the children of Lot," that is, to Moab and Ammon (v. 8). The biblical Hebrew literally states that Assyria has become "an arm" to Lot's descendants. The great empire stretched over the territory of several modern countries, including western Iran, parts of Turkey, most of Syria, and even very briefly along Egypt's Nile River. But it was centered in what is today Iraq, with its capital, Nineveh, situated on the banks of the Tigris River.

Iraq played a very active role in the 1948 and 1967 Mideast wars. It was mainly a supporting role, however, with Baghdad's forces bolstering those of Jordan and Syria. In that sense, Assyria's modern equivalent was literally acting as a "helpful arm" to the eastern front-line Arab states.

In summary, the modern countries where the ten ancient people groups were once situated are Saudi Arabia, Jordan, Lebanon, the Lord's land itself, Iraq, and probably Syria. Arabs from each of these areas took part in Israel's two most important modern wars. There is no historical evidence that these nation groups ever banded together in an ancient conspiracy to wipe out Israel, but all have participated in more recent attempts to do so.

Was Psalm 83 fulfilled in the 1948 and 1967 Arab-Israeli wars? I believe the answer is no. While both conflicts may have been partial or prefulfillments of Asaph's prophecy, a critical piece of those military alliances is missing in Asaph's psalm. Indisputably, the main Arab power that led the others in 1948 and 1967 was Egypt. Yet the North African nation where the Jews were first enslaved is not even mentioned in Asaph's detailed list. While modern Syria can be realistically included, given

that its territory was an integral part of the Assyrian empire, Nineveh's forces only very briefly occupied Egypt. If Psalm 83 is referring to Israel's Independence and Six-Day wars, then the leading Arab military power has been left out.

Egypt's omission from the list is the overriding reason why I think Asaph's regional military conspiracy is still a future occurrence. And given that Zechariah 12 seems to speak of *two* major end-time attacks on Jerusalem—one a localized assault and a second involving all the countries on earth—I suspect that Psalm 83 is probably an outline for Israel's next major war.

Why is Egypt left off of Asaph's list of enemies? Although it would have seemed far-fetched when Zola Levitt and Tom McCall were writing their book in 1974, we all know the transparent answer today. After playing

92

a crucial role in the Soviet-backed Yom Kippur surprise attack on Israel, Egyptian President Anwar Sadat kicked the Russians out of his starving country and invited the wealthy Americans in. That stunning move was followed by the Camp David peace process, which led to a stable, if frigid, peace between Cairo and Jerusalem.

Proving that it was not just a flash in the pan, the Egyptian-Israeli peace treaty is now over two decades old. It survived the controversial Lebanon war and the first Palestinian uprising. Egypt could, of course, scrap the treaty at any time and return to the warpath, as various Egyptian officials over the years have hinted they might do. Pressure to do just that intensified after the new Palestinian uprising began. The burgeoning country is awash with sophisticated weapons purchased under U.S. tutelage. But the financial and political costs of returning to the warpath would be enormous for a government struggling to feed an exploding population.

Besides the mammoth largess of American foreign aid that flowed into Egypt following the Camp David signing, there is another reason that Sadat made peace with Israel in 1978. The Russians helped Gamal Nasser, the powerful Egyptian strongman, build a giant dam on the upper stretches of the Nile River in the late 1960s. The Aswan High Dam was meant to stop regular flooding of the teeming Nile valley and delta regions, where almost all Egyptians live. The concrete dam succeeded in stopping the floods, but it also provided Israel with an astonishing strategic gift. The Six-Day War showed beyond a doubt that the dam is well within reach of the famed Israeli Air Force. Destroying the dam would send a wall of water crashing into Cairo and other cities, something that is never far from the minds of Egyptian military planners.

The alliance described by Asaph is formidable even without Egypt. It includes some of the most heavily

93

armed nations on earth. Let's take a closer look at the modern countries that comprise his "enemies" list.

Saudi Arabia has never sent troops to battle against Israel, but it has always provided moral, financial, and equipment support to the front-line confrontation states. It may play that role again in Psalm 83's war, or it may be directly involved. Some Israeli military strategists believe, or at least hope, that the oil-rich government in Riyadh is too business-oriented to join in an attack on the Jewish state. After all, the desert country is the world's largest single oil producer, and most of its customers and contracts are in the West. It has also supported, albeit indirectly, the Oslo peace process. Yet Israeli officials are well aware that the Saudi regime is the guardian of Islam's most sacred sites on earth and cannot ignore widespread Muslim antipathy to Israel.

With petrol dollars inundating Saudi coffers, the government went on a military buying spree in the mid–1970s. Over sixty-three billion dollars were spent in just the seven years before the preliminary Oslo accord was signed in 1993. The Saudis also doled out a couple billion dollars for Iraqi military purchases before the Gulf War and financed weapons for Syria before and after the conflict. Among other things, Saudi aid has been used by Damascus to purchase North Korean–made Scud missiles. The desert kingdom also helped finance the PLO, especially before Saddam Hussein's invasion of Kuwait.

The United States and other countries gleefully offered to sell some of their most sophisticated weapons to the wealthy Saudi regime, including over 150 American F-15 jet fighters, British Tornadoes, and AWACS command and control jets. The warplanes can easily strike Israeli targets, especially from the Tabuk air base in northwestern Saudi Arabia. Israeli officials protested in 1992 when President George Bush announced the latest F-15 sale (of seventy-two advanced McDonnel-Douglas F-15 XP jets), saying their potential use would tie up Israeli forces in the south even if the Saudis stayed out of any future Mideast war. More ominously, Riyadh has reportedly purchased sophisticated Chinese missile systems that can blast Israeli civilian centers.

The second country that fits Asaph's enemy list is Jordan. The Hashemite kingdom has, as noted earlier, been a key player in previous Arab-Israeli wars. But now it has made peace with its Jewish cousins. Actually, that is not quite the case. It was the former leader of Jordan, the highly esteemed King Hussein, who officially buried the hatchet. Benevolent though he was, the king was basically a dictator whose word was his people's uncontestable command. Many groups, including workers unions representing the legal and media professions, protested verbally against the 1994 U.S.–sponsored peace treaty. Islamic groups also expressed strong opposition to the accord. But the treaty sailed through the Jordanian parliament, whose members would have been sent packing if they had stood in the way of the supreme leader's wishes.

Now commanded by King Abdullah, Hussein's untested young son, Jordanian forces are no match for Israel's. Still, the kingdom has by far the longest shared border with the small Jewish state, making it a serious threat in any regional conflict. Also, Amman is only seventy miles east of Jerusalem. Air force jets can make the journey in minutes.

The most frightening scenario for Israeli military planners—and an increasingly likely one as the new Palestinian uprising unfolds—is an Iraqi military sweep into Abdullah's sparsely populated kingdom, bringing Baghdad's forces to within easy striking distance of Israel's population centers. This could occur either with or without the king's consent. Another scenario is a

Palestinian takeover of the government in Amman (a majority of Jordanians are of Palestinian origin, and the PLO already attempted such a coup in 1970). A Palestinian revolt could be concurrent with or followed by an invitation for Iraqi military backing. Yasser Arafat stood behind his buddy Saddam Hussein during the Gulf War, and the Palestinians maintain close links to Baghdad. (Saddam returned Arafat's favor by calling for a full-scale Islamic holy war against Israel at the emergency Arab summit meeting in October 2000, pledging to send four million volunteer fighters into battle.) Such an invitation for help would literally fulfill Asaph's statement that Assyria had become "an arm" extending assistance to Amman.

The Palestinians themselves are likely to remain hostile toward Israel even if they eventually secure actual sovereign control over Jerusalem's Old City. Animosities run so deep that the Palestinian leadership would be tempted to board any threatening war train that comes along. While they do not pose an existential threat to Israel, Palestinian security forces and rioting civilians could tie up many soldiers and equipment in any new regional conflagration.

Lebanon has virtually no military muscle to speak of. Still, Israel's northern border region has long been the recipient of rockets, artillery shells, and terror attacks launched by various forces operating in south Lebanon. The Land of the Cedars can be expected to play host to more such assaults in any future conflict. Most worrisome are Iranian-backed Hizbullah militiamen who possess rockets that can readily reach the populous Haifa area, Tiberius, and the Galilee panhandle, possibly armed with chemical warheads.

A new Mideast war is almost inconceivable without Syrian participation. Damascus has an arsenal of weapons that nearly matches all of the other listed nations combined. Syria's standing army is estimated to be about three times the size of Israel's, and its tank and artillery forces, while substantially older than Israel's, are numerically much larger.

In recent decades, Syria has acquired advanced warplanes and anti-aircraft missile systems from Moscow. But the main threat posed by Damascus is its substantial ballistic missile capability. Israeli analysts estimate that the country can deploy up to one thousand independently targeted warheads. North Korean–built missiles have poured into Damascus airport, and the rogue Communist state has even licensed local production of Scud-C missiles, an improved version of the ones shot at Tel Aviv by Saddam Hussein. The prospect of such weapons striking Israeli targets is made more gruesome by the likelihood that they would carry chemical payloads. Syria is known to be producing VX nerve gas, one of the deadliest chemical agents on earth.

DESTRUCTION OF DAMASCUS

Two separate prophecies seem to indicate that Syria and Israel will fight a decisive war in the end times, a war that will be catastrophic for Damascus and highly damaging to Israel. According to a prophecy in Isaiah 17, the Syrian capital will be entirely obliterated. The great Hebrew seer foretold that Damascus would be "removed from being a city" and become "a fallen ruin" (v. 1). This has never actually occurred, say historians, with Damascus currently the home of several million people. Surrounding cities will then become uninhabited, with only animal flocks passing through them (v. 2). Sovereignty will disappear from Syria's capital, and military fortifications will no longer be considered necessary by residents of Ephraim—a biblical name for

97

areas north of Jerusalem (v. 3). Meanwhile, Jacob's "fatness . . . will become lean" as his previous glory fades (v. 4). Israel will be stripped as by a reaper but not completely destroyed (vv. 5–6).

The twin prophecy to the one detailed above is found in Jeremiah 49:23–27. A day will come when Damascus will become helpless and gripped with panic and distress (v. 24). It would have been better for the city if it had been totally evacuated (v. 5). Her young men will fall dead in the streets, and all the men of war will be silenced (v. 26). Then fire will burn the stone walls of Damascus—an apocalyptic scene indeed.

Bible scholars are not aware of any ancient fulfillment of Jeremiah's jarring prophecy, although some say it is conceivable that it could have occurred and gone unrecorded. All agree, however, that Isaiah's prophecy was never literally fulfilled. Damascus was certainly never completely annihilated as described, although Israel and Judea were virtually wiped out during the Assyrian and Babylonian invasions. Neither war emanated from Damascus nor caused such grave repercussions for Syria.

Several other strong hints indicate that this is a future, end-time prophecy. One is found in Isaiah 17:3, where God declares that "the remnant of Aram" will be "like the glory of the sons of Israel." Aram is another name for Syria, derived from the ancient Aramaeans who lived there. This revelation parallels Isaiah's prophecies elsewhere that a redeemed remnant will emerge from Egypt and Iraq, which will worship the Lord hand in hand with the Jewish people in Jerusalem (Isa. 19:23–24), and that a spiritual awakening will one day sweep through Lebanon (Isa. 29:17–21).

Isaiah reveals that the destruction of Damascus and the stripping down of Israel will occur in an era when "man will have regard for his Maker, and his eyes will look to the Holy One of Israel" (17:7). This closely corresponds with his earlier prophecy that many nations will seek the God of Jacob in Jerusalem in the last days (2:2–3).

Another hint that this is an end-time oracle is found in Isaiah 17:6, where we are told that Israel will be struck "like the shaking [literally, "striking"] of an olive tree." This unique analogy is used in only one other place by the prophet, 24:13. There, however, it is the entire earth that is violently shaken during God's final judgment of sinful humanity, which is vividly described throughout the chapter.

Isaiah foretells that the nations will be in an "uproar" at the time that the Damascus prophecy is fulfilled (17:12), but God will rebuke them and they will flee far away. Nonetheless, he will pursue them like "whirling dust before a gale" (v. 13). Interestingly, Asaph had earlier called upon the Lord to pursue Israel's enemies, making them "like the whirling dust, like chaff before the wind" (Ps. 83:13).

The apparent Syria-Israel clash described in Isaiah 17 could be part of the regional conflict described in Psalm 83, or it might precede or even follow it. I tend to think—as I indicated in *The End of Days*—that it will probably precede, and even be a catalyst for, the prophesied Psalm 83 attempt to destroy Israel. If so, this battle could actually be Israel's next war, although I suspect the Psalm 83 assault will be closely linked, if not concurrent, with it. The regional conflict might follow in the immediate wake of a Syrian clash with Israel, or be a delayed response to it. As I stated before, Syria is possibly included in the Psalm 83 conspiracy under the name Assyria, but not definitely so.

The forecast destruction of Damascus could be a supernatural occurrence carried out directly by the powerful arm of the Lord. We know from other Scripture passages, however, that Israel's God often uses His people to execute His divine punishment decrees. Could it be that Israel will one day set the walls of Damascus ablaze, causing Syrian troops to fall down dead in the city's streets and making the area humanly uninhabitable? We all know that nuclear weapons can quickly produce such results, as can massive conventional bombing. Could it be that Israel might be attacked by chemical or other nonconventional weapons, leading to a horrible "striking" of many of its citizens, followed by a nuclear response against Damascus? Only God knows at this point. Maybe He Himself will pour out a supernatural judgment for which the nations will blame Israel. One thing is certain: An atomic bomb attack on the sprawling ancient city—one of the most important capitals in the Muslim world—would literally transform it into "whirling dust in the wind." It would also set off an international eruption of condemnation against the beleaguered Jewish state, even if it was justifiably responding to a chemical attack.

While speaking about this prophecy at various international venues, I have enountered protests that a loving God could not possibly allow an entire city to be wiped out in such a deplorable manner. My only answer to that heartfelt contention is Isaiah 24, which reveals that *the entire earth* will be "completely laid waste and completely despoiled" during the final end-time judgment (v. 3). The prophesied fall of Damascus may just be the initial warning of what lies ahead.

I suspect that Israel's next major war will involve the nations that Asaph named in Psalm 83 and that the outcome will be as described in Isaiah 17. Israel will be greatly humbled but not destroyed. The defeat of her enemies will be so stunning that it will cause some of them to seek the God of Israel. Meanwhile, the nations will be in an uproar against the Jewish state (this would definitely be the case if the main victims of Hitler's Holocaust were the first since World War II to let the nuclear genie out of the bottle). The stage would be set for the final Antichrist world ruler to enter the picture.

Despite this rather grim prospect of ghastly warfare ahead, Jews and Gentiles alike can take heart that our God is full of mercy and compassion. He will protect and deliver His people. He will even show mercy to any enemy who truly repents.

Understanding God's propensity for forgiveness, Asaph ends his psalm by imploring the Almighty to fill Israel's enemies with dishonor so that "they may seek Thy name O LORD" (83:16). Then, in their abasement and shame, they too will know that "Thou alone, whose name is the LORD, art the Most High over all the earth" (v. 18). May our gracious heavenly Father have mercy on Israel in her coming battles—and on us all!

6

The End-Time Temple

The most frequently asked questions I receive from Christians while traveling around the world concern the rebuilding of a Jewish temple in Jerusalem. Do I think an illustrious new edifice will rise up on the site of the former temples? If so, who will build it, and when might construction commence? A second set of questions focuses on the sacred ark of the covenant that once sat inside the inner Holy of Holies. Has it been found underneath the Temple Mount in the Old City, as many reports maintain, or possibly next to the Garden Tomb? What about published reports that it has been located in Ethiopia, Petra, or somewhere else in the Middle East or Africa?

I began this book by noting that I am not a trained Bible scholar. Here, I must point out that I am hardly a professional archaeologist or historian. I do, however, have friends who work in those fields, and they have helped me to develop informed opinions on the above questions. My private study of the Scriptures has also played a significant role in the formation of my views, as has my longtime residence in Israel.

Let me start by saying how privileged I am to have lived for many years in a Jerusalem neighborhood that lies due south of the ancient Temple Mount. In fact, my apartment is located on the exact north-south line that runs through the site where the sacred temples once stood. The only road from my neighborhood into the center of modern Jerusalem passes along a ridge that overlooks the entire city. Because of the spectacular view, the barren ridge was transformed into a popular stone-faced promenade soon after I moved here in the mid–1980s. When the weather is fine, as it usually is, the promenade is often packed with tourists and local residents alike. All come to enjoy the panoramic view of the Lord's beautiful contested holy city.

I have walked up to the nearby ridge many times over the years, especially to pray for Jerusalem. The place where I usually sit, in a small pine tree forest next to the promenade, is the spot where Jordanian forces began shelling the western part of the city at the start of the Six-Day War. I sit in front of a sprawling fenced complex that currently serves as Mideast headquarters for the United Nations but housed the British Mandatory administration offices until 1948.

To say the least, it is an inspiring place to pray. On a very clear day, I can see the barren hills of Jordan above the Dead Sea to the east. One can actually make out the distant lights of Amman on a cloudless evening. Just a couple of miles to the northeast lies the historic Mount of Olives, featuring two prominent stone-faced towers— one atop a German-built hospital and the other marking the traditional spot where the Messiah ascended from earth to heaven nearly two thousand years ago. A modern communications tower protrudes from Hebrew University's Mount Scopus campus just north of the Mount of Olives. The mosaic-faced Church of All Nations is visible in the Garden of Gethsemane, tucked away in the Kidron valley at the base of the hill. The southwestern slopes of the Mount of Olives are covered by a large Jewish cemetery, testifying to the fact that the area is hallowed ground to the Israeli people. Among the thousands of Jews buried there is the late Prime Minister Menachem Begin.

Rising up from the deep Hinnom valley straight ahead of where I sit is the matchless walled Old City. In its southeast corner sits the rectangular Temple Mount and the adjacent Jewish Quarter. Two Islamic shrines, the Dome of the Rock and Al-Aksa mosque, dominate the disputed site, proclaiming the triumph of Islam in previous battles over the city. The pure gold roof of the Dome of the Rock shrine—paid for by the late King Hussein and worth millions of dollars—glitters in the sunshine, as it does under floodlights at night. Distant groups of penitent Jews can just barely be discerned along the ancient Western Wall of the Temple Mount, crying out to God to restore the entire hallowed hill to the Jewish people. The grayish dome of the Church of the Holy Sepulchre rises west of that, along with various church steeples scattered throughout the Christian Quarter. Further west, beyond the Old City walls, modern skyscrapers housing hotels and offices rise into the air, affirming that the antique Old City is now just a small portion of rebuilt Jerusalem.

With such an awesome scene before me, I usually meditate on what went on in my adopted hometown in days gone by. On these dusty hills, Abraham, Isaac, and Jacob walked after having been promised that the entire

105

land would belong to their offspring one day. Here King David defeated the Jebusites and established his royal throne. Just above the walled Hinnom valley town, his son Solomon built the first temple to the mighty God of Israel. After scores of prophets, priests, and kings strolled upon its venerated stones, the Lord's sacred house was destroyed by the Babylonians and then rebuilt by Ezra, Nehemiah, and company.

In this very city, the toddler Yeshua was brought by His mother Miriam and Yoseph (Mary and Joseph) to be dedicated to God in Herod's magnificent renovated temple. As a grown man, the Son of David turned over moneychanger stalls in the temple courtyard and then prophesied from the nearby Mount of Olives that not one stone would be left upon another; they would all be torn down. In the olive tree garden still visible just below the Old City in front of my eyes, Yeshua was arrested. He was later tried in the Old City and then crucified somewhere just outside the ancient walls.

Three days later the slain Messiah stunned His disciples and began a spiritual revolution by rising up from the grave. Weeks later He ascended into heaven from on top of the Mount of Olives. Some days after that on the Temple Mount, the Holy Spirit was poured out on the Lord's seemingly leaderless flock. Later still, a rabbi named Saul set about to persecute the growing numbers of believers in the city. After his Damascus conversion, he ignited a riot by proclaiming his spiritual rebirth on the Temple Mount. Within a few years, Roman forces set the city ablaze, destroying Herod's temple and ending a millennium of Jewish prayer on top of the holy hill.

When I visit my favorite prayer spot, I don't just dwell on the past, momentous as it was in Jerusalem. Increasingly I find myself picturing the future of the sacred landscape before me. I try to visualize rivers of fresh water cascading out from underneath the Temple Mount, flowing down into the Jordan valley in front of me, and then turning eastward toward the Dead Sea. I imagine the Mount of Olives split down the middle and the precious feet of the Messiah touching down upon it, with thousands of angels and saints following in His train. I envision the Temple Mount rising up above all the hills around it, including the one that I live on south of the Old City. Sometimes I think about the New Jerusalem that Revelation 21:10 tells us will one day descend from heaven to replace the old. If the city's past was like no other place on earth, what can compare to its prophesied glorious future?

Yet sometimes I weep for Jerusalem, as my beloved Master did two thousand years ago. It is not just a place of historic pain and struggle; it is a hurting city today. The Jerusalem above is free; she is our mother. But the city below is in heavy chains with her children at this very hour.

As a journalist, I have covered riots and terror attacks in the remarkable place I call home. The first violent Palestinian uprising raged between late 1987 and 1993 in many parts of Jerusalem, including the Arab neighborhood right next door to mine. I've heard the screams, inhaled the tear gas, and ducked the bullets—just like so many others in this contested city. I have stood in gatherings of angry Palestinians demanding that Israel hand over the eastern half of Jerusalem. I have waded through crowds of irate Israelis denouncing the latest terrorist outrage that destroyed a city bus, vegetable stalls, parked cars, or shops and restaurants. I've conversed with drug addicts looking for change at busy intersections and driven past prostitutes selling their bodies late at night next to city bus stops. This too is the Jerusalem I see when I look out from my vaulted vantage point.

I also sometimes pray for God's perfect will to be done concerning a rebuilt Jewish temple. I vividly recall the deadly riot that broke out on the Temple Mount in 1990 when a fringe Israeli group attempted to lay a cornerstone for a new temple. I am frankly quite wary of Jewish or Christian groups who are seemingly attempting to force the hand of God on this most volatile issue. There are over a billion Muslims alive on planet earth today, and many will not take kindly to any endeavor to change the status quo on what they call the Noble Sanctuary. When one speaks in Jerusalem about a rebuilt temple, it is wise to remember that the walls have ears. It is far from being a mere academic issue in the modern, expanding city of the great King.

WHAT DO THE SCRIPTURES SAY?

I am convinced that the sacred Jewish and Christian Scriptures solidly indicate that an end-time temple will indeed be constructed on the Old City's venerated Temple Mount. I will explain my conclusion in the following paragraphs. I have enormous doubts, however, that it will be Israel that initiates the building of a new temple, even though this is by far the most popular view among evangelical and charismatic Christians.

The projected edifice is often dubbed the Third Temple, although many scholars deem Herod's renovations to have been so substantial that they call his finished product by that name. Whatever we term it, the Bible seems to clearly reveal that some sort of religious structure will be present on the Temple Mount in the last days. The evidence is found in both the Old and New Testaments. Let us begin with the Book of Daniel.

The prophet Daniel did not have the distinct privilege of prognosticating in Jerusalem. He was already in far-away Babylon with most of his exiled countrymen when the word of the Lord came to him. Unlike the other Hebrew seers, he could only imagine Zion, yet he longed for it as a deer pants for water. Possibly his exilic position was why his book has been relegated in the Hebrew Bible canon to the "writings" section and not to the prophets' portion.

While he may not have held the official office of a prophet, there is no disputing that Daniel prognosticated some of the most important things found in the Bible. It was he who saw in a vision "one like a Son of Man" coming on the clouds to be presented before "the Ancient of Days" (7:13). This Son of Man was then given "dominion, glory and a kingdom, that all the peoples, nations and languages might serve Him" (v. 14). Daniel then reveals that this Son of Man's dominion "will not pass away; and His kingdom is one which will not be destroyed" (v. 14).

But the bulk of Daniel's revelations deal with the final years of human history, just before the Son of Man descends from the sky to rule in glory. The oracles Daniel recorded did not generally come directly to the prophet-statesman in word form. Some unfolded as God gave him the interpretation of King Nebuchadnezzar's dreams. Others were contained in personal visions that were explained by the angel Gabriel.

These interpretations revealed that four great empires would rule over the known world. The last one, the Roman empire, would be the most powerful. It would destroy the city of Jerusalem and its sacred sanctuary. Later a final world leader would emerge from its roots. His power would be unrivaled as he altered laws and attempted to crush the saints of God. But his kingdom would be utterly destroyed, replaced by the everlasting rule of a holy God.

The last two chapters of Daniel are the ones that contain information connected to an end-time temple. The information was revealed to Daniel by an exalted figure who appeared to him by the banks of the Tigris River (10:4–5). The man's face glowed like lightning, and his words were as powerful as thunder (v. 6). Christian scholars generally call this a "theophany," a preincarnate appearance of the Lord, such as Ezekiel records in the first chapter of his book.

The Lord reveals a series of future events that will end with an unprecedented time of distress for Israel (12:1), followed by the resurrection of the dead to either eternal life or to everlasting contempt (v. 2). The contents of chapter 12 establish without doubt that some of the occurrences described in the previous chapter are end-time happenings as well.

The beginning of chapter 11, however, speaks with remarkable accuracy of historical events that occurred in ancient times, such as the conquest of the Persian empire by Alexander the Great and the subsequent breakup of the sprawling Greek empire after Alexander's death (vv. 3–4). Other prophetic details concern his successors in the eastern portion of the fragmented Greek federation and their battles with Egypt.

Scholars generally believe that Daniel 11:21–35 refers to Antiochus Epiphanes, the Greek-Syrian ruler who desecrated the Jerusalem temple in 168 B.C. by slaughtering a pig and setting up a statue of Zeus inside the Holy of Holies. This is referred to in verse 31 as the "abomination of desolation." But many experts believe that the latter part of this section also looks forward to the final Antichrist world ruler spoken of earlier by Daniel and also in the New Testament. In particular, verse 31 seems to have a dual fulfillment.

Verse 36 and subsequent verses carry on with a description of the defiler who does away with the regular sacrifice and sets up the abomination of desolation as Antiochus did. But the description does not at all match the historical record of the Greek-Syrian leader's post-desecration actions or death. Therefore, another defilement seems to be in view. This is strongly supported by the words of Yeshua Himself, delivered to His disciples on the Mount of Olives just before His crucifixion and resurrection. He plainly refers to the "abomination of desolation which was spoken of through Daniel the prophet" as a future event (Matt. 24:15).

Some scholars insist that the Lord's prophecy was fulfilled about four decades later when Roman soldiers destroyed the temple, as Daniel 9:26 foretold. But there is no indication that the empire's forces set up any desecrating object inside the holy house. Also, Yeshua went on to detail a time of unprecedented worldwide upheaval and persecution for the residents of Jerusalem. While they did suffer tremendously during the Roman military operation, the Lord further linked this "great tribulation" with catastrophic earthly and heavenly events that would usher in His triumphant return (Matt. 24:16–31). So the abomination of desolation that He referred to must be a future occurrence.

It is precisely Yeshua's words that cause me to state unequivocally that an end-time temple will be built in Jerusalem. His statement, as Matthew recorded it, was this: "Therefore when you see the ABOMINATION OF DESOLATION which was spoken of through Daniel the prophet, *standing in the holy place . . .*" (24:15, italics mine). Mark's version is slightly different but essentially the same: "But when you see the ABOMINATION OF DESOLATION *standing where it should not be . . .*" (Mark 13:14, italics mine). What the Lord probably said was "standing in the holy place, where it should not be." At any rate, the words "holy place" could have meant only one thing to His disciples' Jewish ears—the inner sacrosanct chamber of the holy temple. It is a well-known biblical phrase in Hebrew, *ha macom ha kadosh,* literally, "the place, the holy." No other spot on earth could possibly fit Yeshua's words.

How can such an abomination be raised up in "the holy place" if there is no Jerusalem temple? Yet the Lord clearly foretells that the desecrating object spoken of in Daniel 11:31 will be erected *inside* the temple one day. His revelation came just after His devoted followers pointed out the wonderful temple buildings to Him. He undoubtedly shocked them by replying that "not one stone here shall be left upon another, which will not be torn down" (Matt. 24:1–2). So the holy temple would be destroyed—as most certainly took place—and then apparently be rebuilt in order to fulfill the end-time event that Yeshua subsequently described.

The apostle Paul also seems to refer to a rebuilt end-time temple, although this may not have been clear to his readers at the time since Herod's structure was still standing. In his second letter to the Thessalonians, chapter 2, he writes about the Lord's prophesied second coming. He reveals that the saints will be physically gathered to the Lord (v. 1) but not before "the apostasy comes first, and the man of lawlessness is revealed, the son of destruction" (v. 3). He then goes on to echo the more detailed description of the nefarious ruler recorded in Daniel 11:36. Paul says that this lawless man "opposes and exalts himself above every so-called god or object of worship" (2 Thess. 2:4). Daniel 11:36 states that "the king will do as he pleases, and he will exalt and magnify himself above every god, and will speak monstrous things against the God of gods."

Paul added that this blasphemous man will "take his seat in the temple of God, displaying himself as being God" (2 Thess. 2:4). While it is true that the apostle elsewhere referred to the church as the temple of God, it seems apparent here that he is reflecting the prophecy of Daniel 11, which undeniably speaks of the wood and stone edifice in Jerusalem. Moreover, Paul preceded his reference to the temple by revealing that the Antichrist will "take his seat" there. While this could also be metaphorical—foretelling that the man of sin will emerge from the Christian church—its most natural meaning is that he actually sits down inside the holy temple in Jerusalem. After all, that was the spot where the glory of God dwelt on earth, and this pretentious pretender is now claiming to be God.

The final New Testament reference to an end-time temple is found in Revelation 11:1–2. The apostle John is given a measuring rod by an angel and then told to "rise and measure the temple of God, and the altar, and those who worship in it. And leave out the court which is outside the temple and do not measure it, for it has been given to the nations; and they will trample underfoot the holy city for forty-two months."

It is hard to spiritualize the angel's words here, although the Book of Revelation as a whole certainly contains much apocalyptic symbolism. The angel gives John a measuring rod, which presumably means he will be asked to gauge something that can actually be measured, such as a literal building. An altar within the temple is also mentioned, along with human worshipers. A courtyard is located just outside the temple, which was the case with the actual first and second Jerusalem structures. The whole complex apparently lies within Jerusalem, since the non-Jews who are said to be out in the courtyard will "trample under foot the holy city for forty-two months." The "two witnesses" will subsequently be slain in the same city (Rev. 11:7), which is "where also their Lord was crucified" (v. 8). Although many have tried to allegorize these verses as well, they obviously refer to the actual dust and stone city of

Jerusalem. There is no good reason to maintain that the temple mentioned in verses 1 and 2 is anything but an actual, measurable building as well.

WHO WILL BUILD IT?

I trust I have adequately demonstrated that the Bible alludes to some sort of temple that will indeed be situated once again in my adopted hometown. If so, the next logical question is, Who will build it? Here I part company with the prevailing evangelical and charismatic view. I think the biblical evidence is virtually nonexistent that modern Israel will construct a new temple, although it might be natural to assume that the Jewish people are the only ones interested in doing so. As a journalist who has covered the multifaceted, pulsating Jewish state for over two decades, I must say that my intimate knowledge of this land, its inhabitants, and its government leads me to strongly doubt that a temple building project will ever be found on official Israeli drawing boards.

In my international travels, I have discovered that a widespread perception exists among many Christians that the Israeli people are just aching to rebuild their temple. This assumption is fueled by exorbitant Christian media attention to a few small fringe movements that are working for immediate temple construction. I hate to disappoint anyone, but I try to report only the facts, and they are that nothing could be further from the truth.

While the periphery groups are certainly sincere in their fervent desires to see a new temple arise, especially the well-known Temple Mount Faithful group headed by Gershom Solomon, they are nonetheless tiny movements with very little official or public backing. Rabbi

Solomon frequently appears on *Christian* television and radio programs abroad but rarely on Israeli TV. Actually, I did just see him in an Israeli documentary program about the search for the "missing" ark of the covenant, and he was portrayed, as usual, as a dangerous extremist. Most Israelis seem to agree with that characterization. They see Rabbi Solomon and his small band of activist followers as total *meshuganas,* or lunatics. Even many fellow Orthodox Jews who share his deep faith and convictions concerning Judaism's right to build on the Temple Mount find his activist approach either quaint or misguided.

I do want to point out two very positive things connected to the Temple Mount activist groups. They have helped make born-again Christians the world over more keenly aware that the Jewish people are back in Jerusalem to stay and that the prophesied end of days is undoubtedly approaching. The second positive thing is they have forced many Israelis to think about Jewish rights to the venerated site. Indeed, as the Scriptures strongly indicate, the Jewish people will see the restoration of their holy temple at the end of the age. More than this, the Desire of Ages himself will be seated inside of it. So whatever one thinks of their activist approach, Gershom Solomon and others like him help to remind Bible believers that the day of Messiah's epiphany in Jerusalem is looming just over the eastern horizon.

Only some 30 percent of modern Israeli Jews are religiously observant. Of these, only a small portion are actively concerned with the temple question. Most Orthodox rabbis teach that only the Messiah can and should begin temple construction, and it is therefore premature, if not hazardous, to interfere with the issue before he appears.

The basically secular majority has not the slightest interest in a new temple. To the contrary, they view

115

attempts to rebuild it as a barrel of dynamite that could easily spark World War III. The last thing they want to see is a grand building that would not only infuriate their Muslim neighbors but would also strengthen the ultra-Orthodox segment of society. Secular Israelis already chafe under the perceived heavy weight of their religious brethren. Polls show the average citizen feels that his or her country's Orthodox citizens have way too much political power and absorb far too many shekels from public coffers while largely refusing to serve in the armed forces. More to the point, they are seen to be always trying to impose their restrictive lifestyle on secular Jews. Such perceptions are widespread precisely because they are basically true.

Although it may surprise many Christians who have heard Gershom Solomon or others like him speak in a church or via their television sets, the prospect that Israeli government authorities might one day oversee a new temple construction project is anathema to most Orthodox Jews. Only a very few within the minority "modern Orthodox" community—who are usually Zionists unlike most of their black-clad Hassidic brethren—care to countenance such an idea. Most religious Jews find the idea repugnant, preferring that politicians keep their tainted hands off of such a sacred project.

Meanwhile, the secular majority recoil at the thought that the ashes of heifers and smoke of burnt sheep might fill the skies above tourist-orientated modern Jerusalem. They are decidedly more interested in saving whales than casting their sins upon a goat. A new Jewish temple and invigorated Orthodox Zionist sector (the community from which Yitzhak Rabin's assassin came) are about the last things they desire to see. It is only some Christians who imagine that the average Israeli is pining for a rebuilt temple in Jerusalem.

Some argue that a wave of religious piety will sweep over the Promised Land, and that will radically alter majority opinions concerning a new temple. They point to prophecies in Zechariah foretelling that the nation as a whole will repent in the last days. The only problem with such a scenario is that the prophesied mass repentance chronologically seems to *follow* the time when all the nations come up to battle against Jerusalem, which is the last event described before the Lord returns. How would Israel have time to build a temple in those final hours of this era, and how could it house the predicted abomination of desolation, since the desecrating object is apparently erected *before* the final battle takes place?

I am convinced that the Bible verses we examined earlier hold the key to who is most likely to construct a new temple in Jerusalem. Each time the end-time edifice is mentioned, it is in connection with the lawless acts performed by the Antichrist. The only place where this is not transparently the case is in Revelation 11:1–2, but the "beast" is referred to several verses later. Verse 2 records that the nations will trample on the holy city for forty-two months—the exact amount of time the Antichrist will reign according to Revelation 13:5 and other verses.

I am almost certain that it will be the perfidious beast, the man of lawlessness, the son of perdition, the very Antichrist himself, who will order the erection of a temple building in the walled Old City of Jerusalem. He will do so for his purposes: to reconstruct the ancient place of God's resting place on earth so that *he* can sit inside it and blasphemously claim to be that very God—an abominable act indeed! Only he could ignore the shrieks of outrage that would surely rise up from many Muslim fundamentalist quarters. Only he will be strong enough to silence the protests of many infuriated Orthodox

117

Jews, incensed that a foreigner was constructing an imitation of their sacred shrine. After all, "who is like the beast, and who is able to wage war with him?" (Rev. 13:4).

If the Antichrist oversees construction of an end-time temple, will he later permit temple sacrifices to resume, as many Christians believe? I think the best biblical answer is probably not. First of all, most Orthodox Jews would reject the validity of any temple built by foreign hands. I also doubt that the man of sin, who will apparently stand at the apex of some New Age unity religion, would want to permit burnt offerings to ascend to the God of Israel. More than this, the Book of Hebrews states that Yeshua's death at Calvary fulfilled the Father's requirement for a blood atonement sacrifice for humanity's sins. The reinstitution of animal sacrifice would only further hide that spiritual truth from Orthodox Jewish eyes.

But what about Ezekiel's prophecies in chapters 45 and 46 concerning renewed grain and animal sacrifice in the future temple? Christian scholars have argued about that for centuries. Like many of them, I can only point to what Hebrews 9 has to say about the sufficiency of the Lord's once-and-for-all blood offering for our sins.

In terms familiar to him, Ezekiel seems to be outlining the main characteristics of the future kingdom of God, although a rebuilt temple is the focus of the prophecy. The Book of Revelation later transforms these characteristics, including animal sacrifice, into more spiritual images (21:10—22:5).

Some argue that the sacrificial system discussed in Ezekiel's final chapters is far too detailed to be "spiritualized" away. They suggest that it will indeed be reinstated in a millennial temple but with a different purpose than before the death of Yeshua. The ritual animal slaughters would not take away the penalty for sins, but only act as a public way for millennial sinners to have their fellowship with the Lord restored. This could be the case, since this explanation does not seem to violate Hebrews 9. However, any sacrificial system that was reinstated *before* the Lord's return would only act to further obscure what His painful death accomplished for the Jewish people and for the entire world.

Daniel refers to a sacrificial system in several places. The most popular Scripture passage in connection with an end-time temple is found in 9:27, where he records that "he will make a firm covenant with many for one week, but in the middle of the week he will put a stop to sacrifice and grain offering." The remainder of the verse goes on to apparently describe the Antichrist's abomination of desolation.

The outstanding question here is this: Exactly who does the first "he" (the one who makes the firm covenant) refer to? Is "he" the main subject of the previous verses, in other words, the anointed Messiah? Or is "he" the evil prince briefly mentioned in the middle of verse 26? Grammatically speaking, it is far more natural to interpret the first part of verse 27 as referring to the main player in the previous verses—the Lord—as history shows the early church fathers did in their teachings and writings.

Theologically, it was undeniably Yeshua's sacrificial death in Jerusalem that ended the need for daily temple offerings. At His last Passover supper, the Suffering Servant himself revealed that His shed blood would initiate the new covenant spoken of by Jeremiah. Isn't that same covenant the probable subject of verse 27? Yeshua's death ended the need for animal sacrifice and grain offerings and actually made them redundant. Is it merely a coincidence that the Jewish temple was destroyed just a few decades after the Lord spoke, ending the sacrificial system to this day?

Both Daniel and Revelation state that the Antichrist will reign for forty-two months, which adds up to exactly three and a half years. That period precisely matches the second half of the "seventieth week" alluded to in verse 27. So it seems most probable to me, and to many others, that this important verse speaks about the promised Messiah, who would confirm God's eternal covenant with Israel and put an end to the sacrificial system. Then it focuses on the abominable prince mentioned in verse 26, who will rule for half a week, or three and a half years.

The English phrase "he will put a stop to" can have a somewhat different sense in the Hebrew language. The word translated "put a stop to" comes from the same three-letter root—*sheen, bet, tav*—found in the word "sabbath." The masculine, singular, future-tense form in verse 27 is the word *yashbeet,* which may be better translated as "he will put to rest," as opposed to "he will put a stop" or "he will halt." In other words, the subject of the verse puts to rest the entire sacrificial system, which is precisely what the Lord did when He laid down His young life in Jerusalem as a free-will offering for our sin.

A similar interpretation can be applied to Daniel 12:11, which is another popular justification for the idea that temple sacrifice will be resumed in the last days. The verse states that there will be 1,290 days, or around three and a half years, between the time that the "regular sacrifice is abolished and the abomination of desolation is set up." But again, is it "abolished" because it has been previously resumed, as many argue, or is a decree simply issued 1,290 days before the abomination is set up that ritual Jewish sacrifice will not be permitted in the Antichrist's temple? A ruler can ban something that is not in current practice but potentially pending. Indeed, some Orthodox Jews might be ready to resume ritual sacrifice in the Antichrist's temple, but the ancient practice associated with the site will be forbidden or done away with.

In summary, I believe there is every biblical reason to believe that a temple of some sort will indeed rise in Jerusalem's walled Old City sometime during these historical last days. Still, it will most likely not be built by Israel nor feature Jewish ritual sacrifice. I realize these conclusions may not sit well with many who have been taught otherwise by good and godly teachers, preachers, and scholars, but I think both the biblical and on-site evidence confirms this to be the case. Of course, if the growing Muslim-Israeli struggle over the Temple Mount is any indication, the best way to find out might simply be to stick around for a while!

THE MISSING ARK

The intriguing questions about the mysterious ark of the covenant make for great television documentaries, but they are too numerous to adequately examine here. Therefore, I will try to hit the highlights. To begin with, I am not surprised that the topic frequently comes up when I travel abroad, since the venerated ark was *the* tangible evidence of God's enduring covenant relationship with His chosen Jewish people.

The sacred ark was a wooden chest overlaid with gold, which God commanded Moses to build (Exod. 25:10–22). The rectangular container held the precious stone tablets with the Ten Commandments inscribed upon them, a golden jar with some heavenly manna inside of it, and Aaron's rod that miraculously budded. It was, of course, a vital component in the Holy of Holies, the inner sanctum of the temple. Its earlier capture by the Philistines turned into an odious experience indeed, while its arrival in Jerusalem was a cause of joyous celebration for King David.

Is the golden ark, wherever it might be, still the greatest physical evidence of God's covenant relationship with His people? I think not. The most telling proof is the worldwide body of Christ. The fact that close to two billion people from every race on earth profess faith in the Jewish Messiah (even if many appear faithless in practice) is a remarkable fulfillment of prophecy. God's sworn covenants remain in effect with His called-out Jewish people, including the special land covenant. Nevertheless, untold millions of "wild" Gentiles have been grafted into the rich olive tree of Israel over the centuries since Yeshua's resurrection. That alone is a powerful testimony of God's enduring existence and awesome power. For Judaism, the ongoing Jewish restoration to the Promised Land is itself solid confirmation that the Lord remains faithful to His ancient promises.

The main reason so many Christians are curious about the ark is that they assume it will be a necessary centerpiece for a restored Jewish temple. But even if it still exists, I suspect it will never be found. I can already hear some of you readers howling in protest over my last statement, convinced that the ark is an integral part of God's end-time plans. Let me challenge you to reconsider that position, based not on the latest supposed revelation by this expert or that archaeologist, preacher, or rabbi, but on the firmest foundation we possess—the enduring Word of God.

The key passages are found in Jeremiah 3. First, the prophet relates God's disappointment in "faithless Israel," who had polluted the land with her harlotry, resulting in exile from it (vv. 1–9). Then he invites his people to repent, saying he will "take you one from a city and two from a family and I will bring you to Zion" (vv. 12–14). Instead of the pending return from Babylon, the final end-time restoration is hinted at. The recovered people will be given "shepherds after My own heart, who will feed you on knowledge and understanding" (v. 15). This echoes other end-time ingathering oracles found elsewhere in Jeremiah and in Ezekiel.

Here comes the clincher. The great prophet relates the Lord's solemn word that when this prophesied repentance and restoration takes place, the archaic ark will no longer be around, nor even be missed! Verse 16 clearly reveals this: "'And it shall be in those days when you are multiplied and increased in the land,' declares the LORD, 'they will say no more, "The ark of the covenant of the LORD.' And it shall not come to mind, nor shall they remember it, nor shall they miss it, nor shall it be made again.'"

So when Israel's final physical and spiritual restoration occurs, the sacred ark will apparently not be part of it. Something greater will outshine the golden chest. Verse 17 tells us what it is—the very presence of Israel's sovereign Lord!

The verse also confirms that the end-time ingathering, and not the return from Babylonian captivity, is in view: "At that time they shall call Jerusalem 'The Throne of the LORD,' and all the nations will be gathered to it, to Jerusalem, for the name of the LORD; nor shall they walk anymore after the stubbornness of their evil heart." This certainly refers to the ultimate Jewish restoration, which ends with Messiah's earthly reign in Jerusalem.

It could be argued that the ark might be rediscovered and placed in a rebuilt Jerusalem temple, then removed when the Lord returns to reign in the holy city. However, the last part of verse 16 seems to preclude this: "nor shall they remember it, nor shall they miss it, nor shall it be made again." It seems that the ancient ark will have been absent for some time before this prophecy is fulfilled. It will have slipped from active memory. It will not be removed from a rebuilt temple when the Lord returns, because it will not be discovered in the first place. The only way to place a facsimile of the original ark in an end-time temple would be to build one, but that apparently will not occur.

It is essential to recognize that many popular conceptions about an end-time temple, and an ark inside of it, are based on exciting and elaborate scenarios that tend to ignore the Bible. If Jeremiah 3:16–17 does not reveal that the ark is history, then what was the Lord saying through the prophet? It is the popular assumption that the Israelis will one day soon rebuild a holy temple and reinstate animal sacrifice and grain offerings in it that makes the uncovering and restitution of the ark seem essential to complete the picture. This intriguing supposition has been fed by colorful archaeologists and adventurers (a couple of whom I have met) who have set off on a search for the gold-plated ark. Our best guide on these matters, however, is not some starry-eyed archaeologist, dreamer, or Hollywood filmmaker, but the indestructible Word of God.

7

Son of Thunder

=

Jerusalem is a great place to meet some real characters. Having lived in this hallowed, harried city since early 1984, I have come across all types of people. Mystics and prophets are a dime a dozen, especially around the Old City. They can especially be found among Protestant Christians and Orthodox Jews (the latter by far the largest religious community in the modern holy city). Muslim eccentrics tend to hang out in Mecca or in Medina where Muhammad is buried.

At least one of the "two witnesses" mentioned in the apocalyptic Book of Revelation shows up in Jerusalem on a fairly regular basis. Sometimes the prophetic pretenders come in pairs, and once we had two sets in town at the same time. I recall that one "anointed witness" came here expecting to locate his prophesied mate. Our eccentric visitors tend to identify themselves as Elijah and/or Moses, although other less popular candidates for the "witness" role have appeared as well.

One self-professed Elijah turned out to be Ernie from Wyoming (for some reason, our unique characters are usually Americans). He was eventually deported for overstaying his tourist visa as many "prophets" have been before him, ironically confirming their supposed "call" in some eyes. Messianic author and speaker Lance Lambert and myself received a faxed letter in the early 1990s revealing that *we* were the two anointed witnesses! While enormously flattered, we decided—after substantial self-reflection and a little help from our wise, God-fearing friends—that the fax was probably not an inspired word from the Lord after all.

Jerusalem also gets more than its fair share of people who claim to be Jesus, Mary, or one of the other New Testament figures. Fortunately, they usually make their declarations while touring with a group, meaning they are normally cared for by the same. Especially disturbed cases and those who travel here alone sometimes end up in a government-run psychiatric hospital with a wing dedicated to "Jerusalem Syndrome" sufferers. The condition, when visitors or local residents seem to lose site of their actual identity and claim to be a biblical character or some other extraordinary personage, was named by noted Israeli psychiatrist Dr. Yair Bar-El (his last name means Son of God in Hebrew!).

I will never forget the time I was lecturing to visiting American college students at a hotel in the Old City's Christian Quarter. Randy, their professor and tour leader, a friend of mine, was missing. When I innocently asked the students where Randy was, they informed me he was "outside in the bus with Jesus." No, he wasn't having a quiet time during my lecture (although some do slip off into dreamland when I speak). Randy was babysitting a chain-smoking student who proclaimed en route to Israel that he was the incarnate Lord of the universe!

A spate of space cadets cropped up as the city was preparing to mark the new millennium. Several of them were connected to a number of sects (naturally comprised mostly of Americans) who said they had come to Jerusalem to await the imminent arrival of Jesus. During 1999, police deported over thirty people, claiming some were planning to stir up trouble in order to help usher in the Messiah.

With the Israeli media full of dire warnings of a pending invasion of millennial loonies, I wrote an opinion article for the *Jerusalem Post* in early 1999. In it I expressed understanding for Jewish wariness over the predicted Christian tourist horde, agreeing that some nuts would surely arrive and that a few might cause serious trouble. I recalled that the last time the Christian calendar went through a millennial change, the violent Crusades closely followed—not exactly the highlight of Jewish (nor European Christian) history. Therefore, I wrote, Israeli apprehension as the year 2000 approached was wholly understandable.

I did question, however, Dr. Bar-El's widely publicized prediction that up to forty thousand Christian pilgrims might require psychiatric treatment during the expected millennial tourist surge, with some eight hundred needing full hospitalization. I noted that many would be European Roman Catholics coming in response to Pope John Paul's declaration of 2000 as a "holy jubilee year," with a special papal blessing granted to all who visited the Lord's tiny land. Such pilgrims were unlikely to see themselves as biblical figures, I wrote, and even if a few did, their clerical tour leaders would take care of them.

127

I also explained that most Western Protestant Christians—the more usual candidates for such religious delusions—understand that the baby Jesus was probably born three or four years before the date that marks His birth on the Gregorian calendar. This meant that the third millennium most likely began around 1996. I also pointed out that most Christians are aware that the Lord Himself revealed that no one would know the exact time of His return, giving the lie to the widely reported contention that millions of Christians expected the end of the world to come in 2000 and wanted to be in Jerusalem for a front-row seat. In the end, the new Palestinian uprising that began in September 2000 essentially killed off tourism altogether, leaving many potential millennial year loonies in other parts of the globe.

Still, Jerusalem is not called the holy city for nothing. Supernaturally informed prophets, many of them also miracle-workers, have indeed crisscrossed the dusty streets of the city. No other single place on earth claims anything like the variety and numbers of such unusual people in its history. Although Moses never visited Jerusalem, almost all of the other Jewish seers and teachers did. For Jews it is also the place of God's holy temple, and for Christians it is the city where the Lord was crucified and rose from the dead. It is unquestionably the most important spiritual location on earth for both Judaism and Christianity, although some Catholics might imagine Rome holds that exalted place.

THE TWO WITNESSES

I have been an avid student of biblical prophecy since becoming a born-again believer in 1974. As a Jerusalem-based foreign correspondent, I have also learned volumes about the contemporary Mideast situation. Combining these two areas of knowledge, I decided to write an end-time novel, published in 1995. My novel was originally titled *The End of the Age*, but that had to be changed after a similar novel with the exact same title hit the shelves a few months later. Reincarnated as *The End of Days*, my book made its second appearance in 1997. The new edition (printed a couple of years before Arnold Schwarzenegger starred in a bizarre he-man-versus-Satan movie by the same name) has been translated into several other languages.

I'm happy to report that many people have expressed appreciation for my novel. Only last night I ran into a visiting Norwegian woman who said that her nonreligious father was moved by the way I blended real information with apocalyptic biblical prophecies. Some have found restored or new faith from reading it, which is a great blessing to me. Others appreciate the realistic, newsy tone I adopted in *The End of Days*, which comes rather easily to a professional journalist. Others particularly liked the messianic characters, based on real people with whom I am acquainted in the Lord's land. The Mideast and global end-time scenario I painted is based on the actual political and military situation in the region and the wider world, as it certainly will be when the prophecies unfold in real time.

Having happily blown my own horn (I should report that I also received some complaints about my novel, especially over the fact that I killed off one of the main characters early on), I have to admit that one aspect of my book has raised some controversy along with the commendations. As I earlier mentioned, the most popular speculative candidates for the two witnesses are Moses and Elijah. Others throw Enoch into the mix. Many see the unidentified duo as symbolic of Israel and the church, or saved Christians alone, or Jewish and Gentile believers, or even two countries like England

129

and America. In *The End of Days,* however, I proposed two candidates who were, well, rather novel.

Before I get into that, I will set the stage for readers who are unfamiliar with Christian apocalyptic teachings and speculations. The Book of Revelation, the last New Testament book, was written by the apostle John while a prisoner of Rome on the small Greek Aegean island of Patmos. As he meditated on spiritual matters one day, the Lord's beloved disciple experienced a spectacular vision concerning the end of this age and the coming kingdom of God. After beholding the exalted Lord in all of His splendorous glory, he was instructed to write down the details of the elaborate vision.

About halfway through the divine revelation, chapter 11 begins with an angel instructing John to measure the temple in Jerusalem. I referred to this briefly in my look at a possible rebuilt Jewish temple. Then, in verse 3, the dynamic duo come into view: "And I will grant authority to my two witnesses, and they will prophesy for twelve hundred and sixty days, clothed in sackcloth." This announcement comes right after John is told that the Gentile nations will trample underfoot the holy city of Jerusalem for forty-two months, meaning that the 1,260 days are probably concurrent with that period of time and with the forty-two months during which the Antichrist will reign (Rev. 13:5).

God's special witnesses will do some fantastic and frightful things, as revealed in 11:5–6:

> And if anyone desires to harm them, fire proceeds out of their mouth and devours their enemies; and if anyone would desire to harm them, in this manner he must be killed. These have the power to shut up the sky, in order that rain may not fall during the days of their prophesying; and they have the power over the waters

to turn them into blood, and to smite the earth with every plague as often as they desire.

In summary, you don't want to mess with these guys—they are fire-breathing biological bombshells!

Yet the Bible says someone will mess with them—"the beast that comes out of the abyss." When the two witnesses have finished their testimony, this evil world ruler will "make war with them, and overcome them and kill them" (Rev. 11:7). In an apparent haughty show of victory, the Antichrist will order their dead bodies left rotting "in the street of the great city which mystically is called Sodom and Egypt, where also their Lord was crucified" (v. 8). The city is, of course, Jerusalem. Its sanctity has been defiled many times in history and will be violated once again when the two holy men are slain in its streets.

The apostle John recorded that the world will rejoice over the public deaths of the prophets whose words and actions "tormented" them, sending gifts to one another in celebration (Rev. 11:10). However, that is hardly the end of the story: "After the three and a half days the breath of life from God came into them, and they stood on their feet; and great fear fell upon those who were beholding them. And they heard a loud voice from heaven saying to them, 'Come up here.' And they went up into heaven in the cloud, and their enemies beheld them" (vv. 11–12).

Talk about a dramatic reversal of fortune! It is the beast who will suffer eternal defeat in the lake of fire and brimstone (Rev. 19:20). The two witnesses will follow their Lord in experiencing an astounding bodily resurrection in Jerusalem, followed by ascensions into heaven. They, and not their enemies, will rejoice with a final shout of victorious celebration!

131

ARE THEY FOR REAL?

As already mentioned, the exact identity of Revelation's two anointed witnesses has been the subject of much debate and conjecture over the nineteen centuries since John recorded his vision. Many have argued that they are not two actual prophets at all, but represent Christians of all generations, or specifically those living in the end-time "great tribulation" period. They point to the fact that the witnesses are called "two olive trees" and "two lampstands that stand before the Lord of all the earth" (Rev. 11:4). Indeed, lampstands are mentioned in Revelation 1:12, where "seven golden lampstands" symbolize the seven regional churches discussed in chapters 2 and 3.

The term "two olive trees" first appears in the Book of Zechariah, where the trees are found on either side of a golden lampstand (4:2–3). When the prophet asks his visiting angel-guide what the lampstand and olive trees represent, he is cryptically told it is "the word of the LORD to Zerubbabel" (who led the Jewish return from Babylon to rebuild the temple). The angel goes on to reveal the enigmatic word: "'Not by might nor by power, but by My Spirit,' says the LORD of hosts" (v. 6). In other words, the objects seem to represent the type of spiritual authority that the two witnesses will possess, whoever they are.

Scripture plainly states that the body of Christ wields significant supernatural power against the devil, but not necessarily in the spectacular fashion portrayed in Revelation 11 or on the silver screen. We haven't seen too many real-life "fire and brimstone" preachers actually call down burning coals out of heaven. In fact, only Elijah performed such pyrotechnics as far as we know. Few if any have fired flames out of their mouths in order to floor their enemies (or for any other reason for that matter). So, argue not a few scholars, the words of Revelation 11:5 must be taken symbolically and thus represent the awesome authority possessed by the Christian church on earth.

Yet the Bible records that Elijah *did* call fire out of heaven. On top of that, a perpetually burning bush accompanied the children of Israel during their prolonged desert wanderings. Dozens of other extraordinary miracles are recorded in the Bible, including the remarkable bodily ascension of Elijah at the end of his ministry and the unparalleled resurrection of Yeshua. In other words, the Bible is full of the supernatural, meaning the appearance of two fire-breathing prophets in the last days is altogether possible.

Another traditional argument against seeing the two witnesses as literal persons has been annihilated in our time. In relating the usual objections, the *New Bible Commentary* (Grand Rapids: Eerdmans, 1970) notes on page 1293 that Revelation says "the whole world will view their martyred forms and rejoice in their subjugation (verse 9), an impossible thought if two individuals in Jerusalem were meant." Well, it may have been impossible before the era of satellites and global television, but now people all around the globe watch live news broadcasts from Jerusalem and elsewhere on a regular basis.

In fact, my adopted hometown is now an international communications hub, with nearly every major media outlet on earth represented here. Live satellite transmissions are a routine daily occurrence. One can also log onto live pictures of the Western Wall over the World Wide Web twenty-four hours a day. Such an important event as a powerful world ruler slaughtering the two extraordinary prophets would be news of the highest order, and CNN, the BBC, and everyone else with correspondents here in Israel would certainly go live to cover it.

God's two anointed end-time witnesses are clearly part of the worldwide community of saved saints. Indeed, I view them as probable leaders of the persecuted flock at the time of the Antichrist's wicked rule. But no solid reason is found in Revelation 11 to take away their personhood and replace it with the corporate body of Christ. The same goes for the unsupportable contention that they represent two countries (usually a remnant of outdated "British-Israel" theology) or Jews and Gentiles.

There is no valid reason to spiritualize the plain biblical account here, which forthrightly states that two individuals will appear in Jerusalem one day wearing sackcloth, preaching the gospel, and calling down judgments upon sinful humanity. As John's account foretold, they will be killed on a city street and then rise from the dead after a specified period of time while the astonished world watches.

Revelation foretells that many other saints will also speak forth the Word of God and suffer persecution during the end-time great tribulation. Some may even perform incredible miraculous exploits by the power of God. At some point, triumphant Christians will be caught up to meet the Lord in the air, even as the two witnesses will be. Still, there is no substantial reason to plant the remnant church, or two nations, races, or movements in the biblical spot evidently occupied by two flesh-and-blood witnesses who die and rise again.

If the two prophets are actual men, as I obviously believe, then exactly who on earth are they? They might be two humble prayer warriors who receive an unimaginable divine calling one day. This is what happened to many of the prophets of old. It certainly was the case with Peter and Andrew, called from their Sea of Galilee fishing nets to follow the Fisher of Men. One thing seems eminently undeniable: They will not be Harold McGrath from Cleveland and Sven Olaf from Stockholm, or Chou Lee from Hong Kong and Abu Banu from Lagos. They will be *Jews,* and most likely Israelis.

So which Jews will they be? Again, they could be two previously unknown fellows (they are definitely not women) who suddenly blow onto the world stage. But traditional speculations have revolved around two of the ancient prophets who return to earth for this unique end-time role. I have no quarrel with this proposition. Under the circumstances, experienced men seem the best candidates to me.

The biblical principle of a prophet returning to earth is established in the Old Testament Book of Malachi 4:5, where God proclaims that He will "send . . . Elijah the prophet before the coming of the great and terrible day of the LORD." This is amplified by Yeshua's statement, recorded in the Gospels, that Elijah already appeared for a second time in the form of John the Baptist yet is still to come again at the end of the age. It is apparent that the Lord did not mean that His beheaded cousin was actually Elijah, but that the Baptist had come in the *spirit and power* of the great prophet.

This establishes an important precedent. The two men described in Revelation 11 may not necessarily be Old Testament prophets. It may be that the Lord's anointed witnesses only operate in the same potent anointing that belonged to Elijah and Moses (who called down plagues upon Egypt similar to the ones described in Revelation 11:6). Of course, it could well be that the two biblical giants will physically return to earth in the last days, as many expect. The Gospels reveal that they already appeared at Yeshua's side during his transfiguration on a Galilee mountain. But they probably did so in a supernatural way, not in their earthly bodies. After all, Moses died and was buried by the Lord in the land of Moab (Deut. 34:5–6). Therefore, he is awaiting his eternal body like everyone else who has "died in the Lord." The New Testament Book of Jude, verse 9, does say that Michael the archangel disputed with the devil over Moses' body. Yet it does not indicate that his departed spirit ever re-entered his earthly remains, which would seemingly be necessary for the great prophet to physically join Elijah on the streets of Jerusalem.

Is John among the Prophets?

As I said at the beginning of this chapter, I proposed in *The End of Days* two rather unique candidates for the twin roles under discussion. My choice wasn't a product of sheer speculation, but was based on several portions of Scripture that I briefly touched upon in my novel. Naturally, some have dismissed my theory out of hand; others have merely chuckled, while quite a few have seriously considered my postulation. Many have asked me to explain my reasoning more fully, which I will do here.

In my novel, I put forward the apostle John himself—the very seer who wrote down the apocalyptic Book of Revelation—as one of God's two anointed witnesses. His strategic partner in my end-time drama was another New Testament figure, albeit a more minor one, the disciple Nathanael. I will say a bit more about him later on.

Before I continue, I must repeat what I often say in public answers to queries about my choice of John. I am not insisting that he is one of the two witnesses and that anyone who contends otherwise is sorely mistaken. I'm just a journalist who is privileged to report from Jerusalem. That does not necessarily make me an expert on biblical eschatology! At any rate, the qualified "experts" disagree with each other on this and about every other matter, so why shouldn't I get up on a soapbox? What I present in the following paragraphs is not meant to be dogmatic, but is only for your consideration (or amusement or consternation, as the case may be). Indeed, it doesn't really matter if we know in advance the identities of the two awesome end-time prophets, or the Bible would have unambiguously informed us.

But maybe sacred Scripture does give us a broad hint who one of the two witnesses is and most have simply missed it. I suspect this is the case, which is why I am including this chapter for your appraisal.

I came to the conclusion that the apostle John may be one of the two prophets while I was working at a Spokane Christian radio station in 1979—my last full year in America. I was sharing a house in those days with two students who attended the same Bible college that I had gone to five years earlier. We would often debate scriptural questions and controversies over shared meals, sharpening our young spiritual minds.

One day we were discussing the contention of many liberal theologians that the Lord had apparently been mistaken when He predicted that some of His followers "would not taste death" until they saw His return in glory. His enigmatic words are found in the latter part of Matthew 16. Yeshua was addressing His closest disciples six days before His luminous transfiguration. They were gathered at a beautiful spot that I often frequented when I lived in the Galilee panhandle. It lies along the Jordan River tributary of Banias that ran through the Roman town of Caesarea Philippi. The three peaks of Mount Hermon rise above the verdant Banias gorge, with one reaching nearly ten thousand feet high. Reminding me a bit of the mountainous Pacific North-west where I grew up, it is one of the most beautiful spots in the Lord's land.

Yeshua reveals to His most intimate followers that He is about to go to Jerusalem in order to suffer many humiliations at the hands of the Jewish authorities. Then He will be put to death (Matt. 16:21). Even though Yeshua also spoke of His subsequent resurrection, Peter rebuked his Master, saying such a cruel death "shall never happen to You" (v. 22).

The Lord heard the voice of Satan in Peter's desperate pleadings and rebuked the misguided apostle. Then He proclaimed that only those who lay down their lives in this world would gain them back for eternity (Matt. 16:24–26). Next He briefly described His ultimate return, saying, "the Son of Man is going to come in the glory of His Father with His angels, and will recompense every man according to his deeds" (v. 27). Finally, He drops His unexpected bombshell: "Truly I say to you, there are some of those who are standing here who *shall not taste death* until they see the Son of Man coming in His kingdom" (v. 28, italics mine).

Slightly different versions appear in the Gospels of Mark and Luke. Mark records Yeshua as saying that there are some listening to Him who "shall not taste death until they see the kingdom of God after it has come with power" (9:1). Luke's account is the simplest of all: "There are some of those standing here who shall not taste death until they see the kingdom of God" (9:27).

In all three versions, the transfiguration immediately follows, prompting many conservative scholars to point to that supernatural event as the fulfillment of Yeshua's words. Certainly those standing near the Lord when His appearance was gloriously—if temporarily—transformed experienced a foretaste of the resplendent "kingdom of God." The problem with this conjecture, however, is that *all* of those who heard Yeshua speak near the Banias

River were presumably still alive a mere six days later. If the Lord's dramatic words were pointing to His imminent transfiguration, it was a rather strange way to announce it.

The same problem emerges with a second popular conservative apologetic, that Yeshua was referring to the outpouring of the Holy Spirit, which took place soon after His bodily ascension. Again, it was just two months or so after He spoke when "tongues of fire" fell upon the assembled disciples in Jerusalem. One of His Caesarea Philippi listeners definitely failed to survive until that dramatic day—Judas Iscariot. Still, we can assume that most if not all others remained alive, making nonsense out of Yeshua's words if they refer to the imminent Pentecost outpouring.

The main problem with these popular arguments is found in Matthew's account. In all three Gospel versions, the Lord was undeniably speaking in the preceding verses about His glorious second coming. In Matthew 16:28, Yeshua explicitly foretells that those who will "not taste death" will remain alive *until* His return to earth. It simply destroys the context to say anything otherwise. That being the case, liberal theologians have rightly pointed to this verse as evidence that the Lord didn't know what He was talking about in that He falsely expected His return to take place within the life span of at least some of His listeners. This seemingly logical view bothered my two Christian roommates and myself, since we could not discover a truly satisfying rebuttal.

I had been mulling over this puzzle just before reading my Bible one morning. Sipping coffee in the kitchen, I began reading the last chapter of the Gospel of John. Although I had read the portion many times before, the printed words virtually leaped off the page.

Having breakfast (as I was) with His disciples on the shores of the Sea of Galilee, the risen Yeshua asks Peter three times if he really loves Him. This seems to reflect the three times that the apostle denied knowing the Lord just prior to Yeshua's crucifixion. After Peter thrice professes his devotion, Yeshua foretells that when Peter grows old, he will be led to a place that he does not wish to go—a prediction, says John 21:19, of Peter's death (tradition says he was martyred on a cross in Rome). Seemingly at an uncharacteristic loss for words, Peter then asks Yeshua what kind of death John will experience. The answer is extremely intriguing: "If I want him to remain until I come, what is that to you? You follow Me!" (v. 22).

Yet again, Yeshua was making a mysterious statement concerning His second coming and—in hindsight—the apparent supernatural longevity of one of His disciples. His recorded remarks are cited by some liberal scholars as yet another place where the Lord mistakenly predicted that His return to earth would fall within the natural lifespan of His Israeli followers. In fact, the verses almost match the Banias sequence in that Peter first engages in a troubling dialogue with Yeshua, followed by the Lord's reference to His second coming, with the added revelation that at least one of His listeners will still be alive to see that thrilling event.

The fact that Yeshua's statement was mystifying to His listeners is revealed in John 21:23: "This saying therefore went out among the brethren that that disciple would not die; yet Jesus did not say to him that he would not die, but only 'If I want him to remain until I come, what is that to you?'" Then, in the closing words of his Gospel account, John clearly identifies himself as the object of these esoteric speculations: "This is the disciple who bears witness of these things, and wrote these things; and we know that his witness is true. And there are also many other things which Jesus did, which if they were written in detail, I suppose that even the world itself would not contain the books which were written" (vv. 24–25).

Why did John, the Lord's especially loved apostle, feel it necessary to include the enigmatic statement about himself if he was only recording the highlights of Yeshua's short but stunning life? Frankly, it seems at first glance like a total waste of space. Notice that John did not really clarify what the risen Lord had in mind. Instead, he repeated Yeshua's intriguing statement after pointing out that Yeshua did not say that John would *never* die, but only apparently prophesied that the apostle would remain alive until the Second Coming.

It would have been amazing news for sure if Yeshua had revealed that John would never die. But it was hardly a big deal if the Lord simply foretold that His beloved apostle would remain alive on earth until His return. That is, it would not have been a big deal if Yeshua had come back to earth in the first century. Now, however, it is nearly two thousand years since the resurrected Lord of glory rose up into heaven from the Mount of Olives, and His devoted followers are still eagerly waiting for His return. Is John eagerly waiting as well?

As the closing chapter of John's Gospel was bouncing around in my brain, and while my morning eggs made their way down to my stomach, it suddenly occurred to me that both the Matthew 16 puzzle and this one could be resolved easily *if John himself* were one of Revelation's two witnesses. The apostle closes his long and inspiring Gospel account by testifying that he has faithfully borne witness of Yeshua's teachings and life. Is it possible that John will testify to the world in truth once again?

I noticed one other thing the next morning that strengthened my growing conviction that the apostle was probably one of the two anointed end-time prophets.

I had decided to put Revelation 11 in context by reading the previous chapter. In it, John sees a strong angel coming out of heaven carrying a little book (10:1–2). The angel then cries out like a roaring lion, which is followed by the voices of "seven peals of thunder" (v. 3). As John was preparing to write down their messages, he was instructed from heaven to "seal up the things which the seven peals of thunder have spoken, and do not write them" (v. 4).

A little later John is told to take the book from the angel's hand (v. 8). As he does so, the angelic being tells him, "Take it, and eat it; and it will make your stomach bitter, but in your mouth it will be sweet as honey" (v. 9). John does as he is told, almost exactly mirroring the prophetic commission that Ezekiel received at the start of his public ministry (Ezek. 3:1–4). What follows is a description of the powerful preaching and supernatural actions of the two witnesses. Could the recorder of the Book of Revelation himself be one of the two anointed men who will prophesy in the streets of modern Jerusalem?

In light of Matthew 16 and John 21, the contents of Revelation 10 strengthened my belief that I was on the right track about the apostle John. After all, a fact must be confirmed by two or three witnesses. For one thing, I had long wondered why John, having heard the words of the "seven peals of thunder," bothered to mention them at all, since he was not allowed to record what they were for our benefit. Maybe he will pull them out of his aged memory and disclose them to the world when he makes his last days reappearance in Jerusalem clothed with the spirit and power of Elijah.

The two witnesses are killed but only at the end of their 1,260-day ministry, which seems to coincide with the Antichrist's rule. If so, then their death and resurrection will signal the end of the beast's insidious reign and the imminent return of the Lord to earth. If John is actually one of Revelation's two prophets (an exciting prospect given that he was so close to the Lord and wrote down the somewhat baffling book on Patmos), it would exactly fulfill Yeshua's indication that His devoted follower would not taste death until the time of the Lord's Second Coming.

In further nonbiblical research, I discovered that many early church authorities believed that John had never died. This was based on the Lord's mysterious words in John 21 and also on the fact that, unlike the other apostles, no credible account exists about his death. I suspect that may be because John did not die.

On the few occasions when I have presented this material publicly, I have been asked the following questions: If John is possibly still alive, where has he been all these years? Of course, I can only speculate. Maybe he has been holed up in some cave on a remote Greek island, although that seems a lonely existence for nearly two millennia. Maybe he settled in some remote part of the globe, or possibly—as church legend maintained—he has wandered around the world over the centuries with his true identity disguised. If so, he must have some sort of arrested aging process or some other God-given ability to stay physically alive. Or perhaps he was "caught up" to heaven like Elijah and there supernaturally preserved until the appointed time of his return. Only God knows for sure if any of this is true. We needn't get too worked up about it; the Lord will reveal all in His good time.

NATHANAEL

Finally, let's briefly look at my second "novel" candidate for one of the two witnesses. I considered pairing

John with either Moses or Elijah, thus lessening the criticism I knew I would receive from many stalwart prophecy buffs. But if I was going to use Yeshua's comment in Matthew 16 as a basis for my induction of John, I needed to come up with another disciple who was also with the Lord at the foot of Mount Hermon on that day. After all, the Messiah had said, "*Some* of you will not taste death," not *one* of you.

I prayed about my speculative choice and then noticed that John was the only New Testament writer to focus any attention on an obscure disciple named Nathanael (*Natan-el* in Hebrew, which means "God gave"). This was despite the strong possibility that Nathanael was actually another name for the apostle called Bartholomew in the three Synoptic Gospels. Whoever he was, Nathanael was one of only seven disciples listed as being near the Sea of Galilee when the Lord spoke His enigmatic words about John's mysterious future (John 21:2).

An incredible exchange occurred between Yeshua and Nathanael when they met for the first time in Galilee. John records that Philip from Bethsaida located his friend Nathanael and excitedly told him, "We have found Him of whom Moses in the Law and also the Prophets wrote, Jesus of Nazareth, the son of Joseph" (1:45). Nathanael then sarcastically asked, "Can any good thing come out of Nazareth?" which probably reflected popular scorn for the small Galilee town. When Yeshua saw Nathanael approaching, He proclaimed, "Behold, an Israelite indeed, in whom is no guile!" (v. 47). Nathanael was quite surprised that the Lord seemed to know him, since they had never met. Yeshua then revealed that He had seen Nathanael "under the fig tree" before Philip encountered him (v. 48).

Nathanael's response is astonishing: "Rabbi, You are the Son of God; You are the King of Israel" (v. 49).

Indeed, he is the first disciple that we know of to verbally proclaim that Yeshua was both Israel's expected Messiah King and the divine Son of God. The Lord's reply to him was equally extraordinary: "Because I said to you that I saw you under the fig tree, do you believe? You shall see greater things than these. Truly, truly, I say to you, you shall see the heavens opened, and the angels of God ascending and descending on the Son of Man" (John 1:50–51).

We have no record of when Nathanael might have witnessed such an amazing thing. Still, since Yeshua was a prophet, we can assume that it must have occurred at some point. The fact that their unusual meeting and conversation occurred at all and that John was careful to detail it in his Gospel account made me wonder about this mysterious disciple. In light of the fact that he was also present for the Sea of Galilee exchange, I choose him for my second prophetic end-time candidate. However, unlike my nomination of John as a potential witness, this is pure speculation with no arguable biblical basis.

One other thing caused me to suspect that the two witnesses will both turn out to be personal disciples of the Lord. Revelation 11:8 says that their dead bodies will lie on a street in Jerusalem "where also *their Lord* was crucified" (italics mine). Of course, it is true that Yeshua is the Lord of all, including Old Testament figures like Moses and Elijah. But the phrase sounds quite intimate here, as if the two slain witnesses actually knew the Savior from Nazareth before he was crucified.

I'm certain that all of this seems nonsensical to some of you reading these words. What is a professional journalist doing writing about such weird and wacky things as undying apostles, wicked world rulers, and future fiery prophets?

In my defense, I can only point out that truth is frequently stranger than fiction. I have personally discovered this more than once while laboring in Jerusalem as a newsman. Life is much harder to grasp than we pretend and the stars much farther away than we can ever actually comprehend.

I do believe with all my heart that a benevolent Creator is ultimately behind our slightly decipherable and fleeting earthly existence. My belief is partly based on defendable evidence but even more so on faith. I also believe that the God of this vast universe has revealed portions of Himself in a best-selling book that appeared through the agency of a grab bag of Jewish writers and prophets. And so I wrote a novel based on some of their relevant words. At any rate, I enjoy novel ideas.

8

The Rapture Question

═══

One of the blessings of living in a historic city like Jerusalem is that many friends and acquaintances from around the world come to visit. Of course, they hardly fly all the way to Israel just to see me or other friends living here. If they are believers in Yeshua, they come to walk where their Savior was born, where He grew up, where He performed His Father's miracles and ministered His word. They especially come to see where He died and rose again, conquering death for all time. Of course, some come here with little spiritual emotion, but they do want to visit various historical and religious sites in the Lord's special land.

I often venture out to meet friends and tourist groups staying at one of the capital's many modern hotels.

Sometimes I catch up with them at King of Kings, a local church congregation visited by many touring pilgrims. After yesterday's service, a visiting journalist from America came up and reintroduced himself to me (we had met briefly at the National Religious Broadcasters convention in Washington, D.C., a few years ago). He informed me that he had read and enjoyed my end-time novel. With the third Christian millennium just getting underway, we then discussed some possible scenarios for Israel's immediate future. I told him my estimation that another regional war probably would occur fairly soon and explained that I thought Psalm 83 could be its general outline. He then asked me where I saw the rapture and the military invasion described in Ezekiel 38 and 39 fitting into the end-time scheme of things. We briefly discussed these topics, along with other portions of Scripture that deal with the restored nation of Israel in the last days.

Since I stuck my neck out and wrote an apocalyptic prophecy novel, I am often asked questions concerning the exact order of end-time events. Nobody in their right mind expects me to have all, or even most, of the answers to such queries. Yet I have certainly formed some firm opinions during nearly three decades of researching the biblical prophecies, with much of that study undertaken in Jerusalem. That being the case, this chapter focuses on one of the most controversial issues surrounding the prophesied end of days, the rapture.

First, I should briefly try to answer a fundamental question that most people ask themselves, if not others, at some point in their lives: Where is the stream of history taking us? The biblical answer is one of breathtaking contrasts. On the one hand, Isaiah 24 foretells that the earth is destined to "reel to and fro like a drunkard" and "be broken asunder" (vv. 20, 19). All the cities will fall and the earth will be burned up, as the sun apparently heats up into what we now call a supernova. Few will be left alive.

Had such an apocalyptic description come from only one of the ancient Hebrew prophets, we might be able to more easily spiritualize it or dismiss it as esoteric and indecipherable. However, this starkly grim picture of the end of time is echoed in many other portions of the Old and New Testaments, climaxing in John's Revelation. If the futuristic prophecies in the Bible are to be taken seriously at all, then the annihilative aspect of many of them must be reckoned with as well—even if it does not fit in nicely with the feel-good spirit of our age.

On the other hand, a majestic King of Kings is coming who will restore Eden's garden paradise to the earth. Chapters 8, 9, and 11 of Isaiah paint an exhilarating picture of the future, when the world's government will rest upon the shoulders of One called Wonderful Counselor, Mighty God, Eternal Father, Prince of Peace. His just and righteous rule will continue to expand forever (9:6–7). There will be no more war or killing in His eternal kingdom (11:9). Indeed, other Scriptures reveal that death itself will be banished, along with all disease, mourning, and tears.

So which is it, massive death and destruction or everlasting bliss? Obviously, the biblical answer is both. But this seeming conundrum baffles many people, including more than one of my Jerusalem-based journalist colleagues.

If one has the honor (or misfortune, as some see it) to work as a foreign correspondent in latter-day Israel, that person must know at least a smidgen about the Bible. Christmas in Bethlehem is always a story, as is Easter in Jerusalem's crowded Old City. Christian-Jewish, Muslim-Jewish, and Christian-Muslim political, spiritual, and physical fights also occasionally spring up, sometimes centered on biblical sites like the Temple Mount or Nazareth. Important archaeological discoveries occasionally make the headlines. Yet a smidgen of accurate biblical knowledge is *all* that many of my reporter colleagues possess, if that. I don't say this to demean anyone; the Bible simply isn't part of most college journalism curriculums.

As the year 2000 approached, international viewers and readers were served up a cacophony of millennial stories that spoke about "doomsday Christian cults" operating in Israel. I chuckled more than once as my mostly secular colleagues tried to make heads or tails out of such perplexing groups, some of whose members I personally know. "They believe the world will end in the year 2000!" or "They insist that the final battle of Armageddon will begin at the stroke of midnight on New Year's Eve!" were a few of the astonished reports I heard or read.

The fact is that most of the world's evangelical and charismatic Christians (easily many hundreds of millions of people), along with not a few Roman Catholics and Orthodox Christians, can be accurately described as waiting for the apocalypse. It is not that most are pining to see the world toss about like a drunk leaving a bar late at night. We like stability as much as the next guy does, if not more. We wait with anticipation for the end of days, because the biblical "doomsday" spells the termination of this fallen, frightful world with its arsenals of nuclear missiles, widespread poverty and hunger, pollution, international terrorism, frequent wars, cancer and heart disease, AIDS epidemic, wife beatings and child molestation, government corruption, ad nauseum. Much more than this, the Bible makes clear that the prophesied end of this age is also the point in time when the eternal Prince of Peace will come with healing in His wings.

Are committed Christians crazy to expect a cataclysmic end of this present sick world, followed by a golden age of unprecedented peace, health, longevity, and prosperity? Possibly so. But at least we are not hopelessly anticipating worldwide disaster like some nonreligious types who are sober and well read enough to discern the ominous writing on the wall. We have taken out an insurance policy: faith in the redeeming power of God through the agency of His suffering Son. We believe our loving, merciful God will see us through the coming storms and ultimately into the pearly gates.

Caught Away

In a millennium 2000 story for CNN, one of my Jerusalem-based colleagues had the dubious task of trying to explain, in just a few words, what the "rapture" is all about. Considering that he has no Christian background, but is Jewish, he actually didn't do such a bad job. The topic came up when he interviewed several visiting American evangelicals outside the Church of the Nativity in Bethlehem. "We are here praising the Lord because we know that the rapture is going to take place at any time," one beaming American woman told him on camera. He then explained, without elaboration, that some Christians believe "they will suddenly disappear" in a prelude to the end of the world.

Indeed, quite a few visiting Christian pilgrims gathered on the Mount of Olives as midnight approached on December 31, 1999. Although news accounts erroneously had them "waiting for Armageddon," some were actually expecting the rapture to occur that night. Needless to say, like so many date-setters before them, they were wrong.

For any reader unfamiliar with Christian jargon, the term *rapture* refers to a thrilling portion of Yeshua's prophesied second coming. It is also known as the "catching away" and the "blessed hope."

The rapture is explained most fully by the apostle Paul. In his first letter to the Corinthians, he speaks of "a mystery: We shall not all sleep, but we shall all be changed, in a moment, in the twinkling of an eye, at the last trumpet; for the trumpet will sound, and the dead will be raised imperishable, and we shall be changed" (15:51–53). Paul is not espousing a totally "Christian" concept, as some modern Jewish commentators assume. A general resurrection of the dead at the end of days is first mentioned in Daniel 12:2, where those who "sleep in the dust of the ground will awake, these to everlasting life, but the others to disgrace and everlasting contempt." Such an end-time resuscitation is also alluded to in other portions of the Hebrew Bible, especially in the Book of Ezekiel.

In 1 Thessalonians 4, Paul adds meat to the verses I just quoted:

> But we do not want you to be uninformed, brethren, about those who are asleep, that you may not grieve, as do the rest who have no hope. For if we believe that Jesus died and rose again, even so God will bring with Him those who have fallen asleep in Jesus. For this we say to you by the word of the Lord, that we who are alive, and remain until the coming of the Lord, shall not precede those who have fallen asleep. For the Lord Himself will descend from heaven with a shout, with the voice of the archangel, and with the trumpet of God; and the dead in Christ shall rise first. Then we who are alive and remain shall be caught up together with them in the clouds to meet the Lord in the air, and thus we shall always be with the Lord.

> verses 13–17

Occasionally an inquirer wants to know whether or not I believe the rapture will take place at all, but mostly I'm asked about the timing of the event. The latter question has long been a hot-button topic in conservative Christian circles. It is not an issue I usually speak or write about, although I could not avoid including a position when I wrote my end-time novel. I will discuss it a bit more fully here.

Paul's teachings, quoted above, are buttressed by Yeshua's own words concerning his second coming in Matthew 24, Mark 13, and Luke 21. First of all, both the Lord and his apostle plainly speak about a literal return to earth. Attempts to spiritualize Yeshua's return have been consistently rejected by church authorities over the centuries. The Book of Acts records that as the Lord bodily rose into the sky above the Mount of Olives in the presence of many of his disciples, two angels appeared to announce, "This Jesus, who has been taken up from you into heaven, will come in just the same way as you have watched Him go into heaven" (1:11). Nothing could be clearer than that.

In today's crazy world, dozens of sects and cults have sprung up that have redefined the Second Coming as an invisible internal affair. According to this view, the Lord comes to reside inside individuals (the New Testament certainly teaches that Yeshua indwells His people by the agency of the Holy Spirit, but that does not at all preclude His physical return to earth). A few mainline denominations have essentially adopted this position, even if unofficially, while others simply ignore the Lord's prophesied return. Some groups, like Theosophists, contend that the "Christ Spirit" comes periodically to dwell in various great religious leaders. All of these alterations and suppositions disregard New Testament Scriptures concerning the Lord's Second Coming.

We who have accepted God's free gift of eternal salvation can rejoice, because the sovereign Lord of the universe is *physically* coming back to earth. It may be morning, it may be noon, it may be evening, it will hopefully be soon. Whenever it occurs, Yeshua emphatically stated that no one, not even Himself, would know the exact timing in advance (Matt. 24:36).

The Lord did, however, indicate that we could recognize the season of His return if we paid attention to the various signs He outlined during His Mount of Olives discourse. Termed "the beginning of birth-pangs" of the coming messianic kingdom, He said these signs would include an upsurge in wars, famines, and earthquakes, plus the appearance of many false religious prophets. Hinting that His return would not quickly follow His then-imminent death and resurrection, the Lord foretold that the gospel of the kingdom would also be "preached in the whole world for a witness to all the nations, and then the end shall come" (Matt. 24:14).

DISCERNING THE TIME

I do not believe that the Scriptures support the popular contention that the Lord will come back in what amounts to a two-phased return. According to most pretribulation scenarios, Yeshua will first appear in a hidden manner to snatch away His spotless bride and then a few years later come back with His saints in a public fashion—witnessed by all the earth—to judge the nations and establish His worldwide reign. This view presents several major problems that I will not get into here, since it would take an entire book to adequately examine the topic, and other people have already written such books.

Suffice it to say that the apostle Paul plainly states that the redeemed saints, both living and dead, will be "caught up" to meet the Lord in the clouds. This unprecedented event will be preceded by the sounding of a trumpet, or a ram's horn, known in Hebrew as a shofar. All agree that this supernatural catching away is the main element of the rapture.

The first reference to the Lord coming in the clouds is found in Daniel 7:13. Quoting directly from the prophet, Yeshua foretold that at the very end of the "great tribulation" period,

> the sun will be darkened, and the moon will not give its light, and the stars will fall from the sky, and the powers of the heavens will be shaken, and then the sign of the Son of Man will appear in the sky, and then all the tribes of the earth will mourn, and they will see the Son of Man coming on the clouds of the sky with power and great glory. And He will send forth His angels with a great trumpet and they will gather together His elect from the four winds, from one end of the sky to the other.
>
> Matthew 24:29–31

To maintain that Paul's rapture account is not exactly parallel to Yeshua's, as the pretribulation position must do, seems far-fetched to me, to say the least. The same elements appear in both: the Lord coming on the clouds, a trumpet sound, and then the gathering of His saints into the clouds. Certainly Yeshua's prophecy indisputably puts this catching away at the *end* of the tribulation period, when great judgments are about to fall upon the earth. He clearly reveals that His coming will not be in secret; it will be "just as lightning comes from the east, and flashes even to the west" (Matt. 24:27). It is during that spectacular return, while the Lord is still hovering over the earth in the clouds, that the angels will sound a trumpet and "gather together His elect."

I briefly touched on another point earlier in this book. Paul wrote in 2 Thessalonians 2:1–3 that "the coming of our Lord Jesus Christ, and our gathering together to Him" (a clear reference to the rapture) would not occur until "the apostasy comes first, and the man of lawlessness is revealed, the son of destruction." Now, for those who hold that the Antichrist was a historical figure who lived in the first century, these verses pose no problem to the pretribulation theory of "imminence," that is, that the rapture can occur at any time without any prophesied events needing to be fulfilled first. However, since most pretribulation rapturists believe that the Man of Sin is yet to come, Paul's teaching surely blows a big hole in the position that the saints will be gathered to the Lord before the Antichrist begins his worldwide rule.

The rapture timing that I think is the most biblically solid has been dubbed the "pre-wrath" position. I came to accept this view about ten years before author Marvin Rosenthal coined the term. It basically sees the "catching away" occurring as the Lord is visibly descending back to earth at the end of the tribulation period but before He pours forth His judgments on the Antichrist's kingdom as detailed in Revelation 16 and 17. Thus, it is prior to the final battle of Armageddon mentioned in 17:13–16 and the other wrathful judgments that the prophets said will shake this rebellious world to its core. The saints will remain with the Lord in the clouds above the earth during the pouring forth of those horrendous judgments, which will apparently take at least several months. Then they will descend with Him to the Mount of Olives, as described in Revelation 19.

Is it important to know when the prophesied rapture will take place? Not really. The main thing to grasp is that the risen Lord *is* coming back to earth some day.

Since the precise timing of the rapture is not a crucial issue (although you would think it is by the way some folks carry on about it), I rarely discuss it during my international speaking tours. I am a bit concerned, however, when I come across Christians who are only dimly aware that the pretribulation position is not the only one out there. Such uninformed people could be in for a rude awakening—and a big jolt to their faith—if the Antichrist appears and the Lord's devoted followers are still running around on the planet, as many Christian teachers and pastors believe will be the case. It is my conviction that all pastors and prophecy teachers should at least inform their charges that other positions exist and are held by many eminent Christian figures. I am certain that it is better to "expect tribulation" in this world, as the Lord said we should do (John 16:33), than to look for a sudden deliverance that may come later than we hope or expect.

I found it a bit alarming to be bombarded with dozens of "imminent rapture" e-mail messages soon after sustained Palestinian-Israeli violence broke out in Israel in September 2000. Having apparently learned nothing from the embarrassingly false expectations that were broadcast around the globe before the new year began just ten months before, the authors generally claimed that the new Mideast crisis meant it was time to close up shop and get ready to go home.

Mind you, I am all for being ready to meet the Lord at any time. Which one of us knows at what hour we may suddenly exit this life? But I am sad to say I found most of the communications far too escapist. Many Christians (especially my fellow Americans) simply won't face the possibility that we believers might experience some of the end-time upheaval described in the Bible. Yes, let us always be ready to meet the Lord in the air. But let us also be ready to be persecuted, and even to die, for His name's sake, for He is entirely worthy.

157

I realize that many readers will strongly disagree with my "pre-wrath" view. The pretribulation rapture position is still the most prevalent among conservative evangelicals and charismatics, at least in America. In fact, I was taught the pretribulation scenario in Bible college as if it were the only one in existence. More recently, I was aware that my end-time novel would have a much better chance of being a bestseller if I included the most popular rapture timing as part of my scenario (the novel actually sold quite well anyway, but nothing like pretribulation blockbusters such as *Left Behind*). However, since I am hardly alone in questioning the pretribulation view, I had to be true to my understanding of the Scriptures, whatever the cost.

You will hear no objections from me if the Lord snatches us away from this warped and decaying world before the foretold final persecution begins. I don't enjoy suffering any more than the next guy, nor do I relish the thought of living through some of the frightening "birth pangs" described by the Lord. Still, does an expectant mother focus on pending delivery pains or on the baby that is nestled in her womb? With God's help, we can endure whatever comes along. Indeed, many believers are being tested by wars, famines, earthquakes, and government-sanctioned persecution at this very moment. Finally, let's remember that it is only the *timing* of Yeshua's second coming that is in question among most committed Christians, not the fact of His return. May He come speedily in our day—whatever day that might be!

9

Rushing toward Eternity

===

If the things I have written about in the previous chapters of this book are even remotely true, then we may indeed be rushing toward the end of time as we know it. Many of the prophecies contained in the Bible seem to indicate that this is the case. Of course, we need to be extremely careful about making specific predictions. Untold numbers of sincere Christians have been disappointed and have even lost their faith when premature or skewed prophetic speculations have failed to materialize. Unbelievers have seized upon misguided speculations to justify their disdain for the Christian faith. No one should make revolutionary decisions or take radical steps based solely on conjecture. We are certainly told to "keep looking up" for the Lord's return but are also instructed to "occupy" on earth until He comes. In God's good timing, everything will work out as He intended and foretold.

As I stressed in *Israel at the Crossroads,* it is also imperative for born-again Christians to keep in mind that the restored Jewish state is a real place with flesh-and-blood people living in it. The Israeli people—stressed out by years of terrorism, wars, and repeated setbacks in the torturous peace process—are a bit nervous over rampant speculation about gigantic battles and world rulers that are prophesied to rumble through their minuscule homeland during earth's final hours. We cannot entirely avoid speaking about such things, nor should we. They are an integral part of the Bible and therefore important to our faith. Nevertheless, we must speak and act with all due respect and sensitivity to the Jewish people, who have been the recurring object of "Christian" hatred, scorn, and persecution over the centuries. Israelis are, as I said, real people with human emotions and sensibilities. They are not just pivotal pieces in some grand prophetic puzzle. Naturally, the same is true of the millions of Arabs in this troubled region as well.

The Bible contains an exciting beginning and an unforgettable end, like any good book should. The beginning was creation. The end will be destruction but then re-creation. In fact, God's Word has a very happy finale, at least for those who know the Lord. The sin-soaked earth will be reborn. We always need to stress this important fact when talking about the gloomier aspects of the end of this age lest we literally scare people to death.

The final period of history—when the prophesied man of lawlessness will gain control over all the world, a Jerusalem temple will be built, intense warfare will engulf the Middle East, and the saints will be caught up to meet the returning Lord in the air—is commonly thought to last at least seven years. This concept is based on interpretations of two portions of Scripture found in Daniel 8 and 9. I, however, think the biblical evidence points to a shorter period of time, as I will briefly try to demonstrate.

In Daniel 8, the Babylon-based prophet is given a vision of a ram and a goat. He is later told that the ram represents the kings of Media and Persia, while the goat symbolizes the kingdom of Greece (8:20–21). Out of the Greek empire, a "rather small horn" will arise and become great (v. 9), causing some of the stars to fall to the earth (v. 10). Indeed, the little horn will blasphemously declare itself equal to God and remove the regular sacrifice from him (v. 11). This evil pretender will trample down the holy temple, with its regular sacrifice suspended for "2,300 evenings and mornings" before being properly restored (v. 14).

Most Bible scholars agree that the number 2,300 should be taken literally here (a Hebrew day begins in the evening, as per Genesis 1). Put more succinctly, the vision is talking about a period of around seven years.

Daniel's vision undeniably predicts the ancient desecration of the Jerusalem temple by the Greek-Syrian leader Antiochus Epiphanes, discussed earlier in this book. Indeed, it is such an accurate picture of what actually took place that many scholars maintain Daniel 8 must have been written after the events occurred. Helping to disprove this skeptical view, the prophet also spoke in 9:26 about the Roman destruction of Jerusalem, an event that all agree definitely followed the appearance of Daniel's prophetic book. Historians say Antiochus launched his siege against the holy city around 171 B.C. The temple was defiled and then finally cleansed and rededicated in 165. Thus, the entire period of conquest and occupation was a period of some seven years, or 2,300 days.

It is certainly valid to argue that, as in other places, the prophecy in view here telescopes into the distant future, providing a foretaste of the Antichrist's abominable actions and rule. Other Scriptures confirm that the end-time beast will position himself in the temple as God and persecute the saints, as his ancient Greek foreshadow did. The reference to "stars falling to the earth" might more accurately reflect the worldwide reach of the final ruler.

As I mentioned earlier in this book, the Antichrist may not necessarily restart and then halt animal sacrifice in Jerusalem, but simply ban the anticipated resumption of the same. Even if he does permit animal sacrifice, the number of days mentioned here—2,300—need not apply to his reign. In fact, we are explicitly told in Revelation 13 that the man of sin will rule for only forty-two months, which is exactly half of seven years.

Daniel 9:24–27 forms the main basis for arguing that the end-time tribulation period will stretch for seven years. Gabriel reveals to the "highly esteemed" prophet, "Seventy weeks have been decreed for your people and your holy city, to finish the transgression, to make an end of sin, to make atonement for iniquity, to bring in everlasting righteousness, to seal up vision and prophecy, and to anoint the most holy place" (v. 24). The Hebrew word translated as "weeks" literally means "sevens," or units of seven.

Verse 25 goes on to disclose that the seventy-week period will begin with the issuing of a decree to rebuild Jerusalem. Then after the sixty-ninth week, "Messiah the Prince" will come, apparently before the final week. After the sixty-ninth week is finished, the Messiah (literally the "Anointed One") will be "cut off and have nothing" (v. 26). Then the "people of the prince who is to come will destroy the city and the sanctuary." This would later prove to be speaking about the Romans.

This intriguing portion of Scripture has been intensely dissected over the centuries. Most scholars agree that a period of 490 years is in view, since "seventy weeks" equals that number of years. Many see this as a symbolic figure, while others take it quite literally. Either way, it is clear that the climax of the seventy weeks will be the establishment of Messiah's reign, with sin atoned for and no more need for prophecy.

The main bone of contention is the final, seventieth week. Has it already been entirely fulfilled as some scholars and teachers maintain, with Yeshua's resurrection bringing the weeks to their prophesied, glorious end? Has it only been partially fulfilled, with a small but vital chunk still remaining to unfold? Or has it not yet come to pass at all?

The main problem with the "already fulfilled" position is the indisputable characteristics of the nearly two thousand years since the Lord's miraculous ascension into heaven. While everlasting righteousness may have legally arrived with His crucifixion, its daily display in the world still largely remains to be seen. Also, while the deliverance of biblical prophecy may have ceased only decades after His resurrection, the fulfillment of dozens of oracles still remains for the future.

The "partial fulfillment" view is that the Lord's Jordan River baptism, which launched His more than three-year public ministry, set in motion the prophesied final week. If so, then He was "cut off," or crucified, in the middle of the seventieth week, which is obviously after the sixty-ninth week, as indicated in Daniel 9:26.

The final position concerning Daniel's seventieth week is the most prevalent one heard today on popular radio and television prophecy programs. In a nutshell, it is that the entire seventieth week still lies ahead. If so, a seven-year period of persecution, upheaval, and tribulation is yet to unfold. Normally, the first half of the week is said to feature the rise of the Antichrist to power—usually thought to be a relatively peaceful time—followed by the setting up of the abomination of desolation in the middle of the seven years. This is said to unleash some three and a half years of "great tribulation," which end with the fiery judgments of God raining down upon the Antichrist and his worldwide followers.

I tend toward the middle view—that the seventieth week was partly fulfilled by the Messiah's ministry and atoning death, with the last half of the week still to come. I think this position fits Daniel's captivating prophecy better than the other two, although none of them is without problems. The "Anointed One" of verse 26 would then be the main subject of verse 27, as He is in previous verses of the prophecy.

Verse 27 is difficult to interpret because it simply states that "he" will make a firm covenant (the Hebrew literally states that "he will strengthen a covenant") with "the many for one week." Is this referring to the main subject of the seventy-weeks prophecy, the anointed Messiah, or to the "prince" whose people will destroy the temple? The Lord certainly confirmed God's covenant with His ancient Jewish people in His public teachings and actions, even if most of His countrymen rejected Him as Messiah. During the intervening centuries, the worldwide Gentile church has been holding center stage. During the end-time tribulation period, however, Israel's prophesied Messiah will apparently turn His attention back to His Jewish cousins in a special way, as confirmed elsewhere in Scripture.

According to the New Testament, it was Yeshua's shed blood that inaugurated the new covenant first spoken of by Jeremiah. In giving His life as a sacrificial lamb, He strengthened, or confirmed, the covenants God made with Abraham, Isaac, and Jacob and with King David.

This "strengthening," or "confirmation," of God's solemn commitments to Israel seems to fit the context of Daniel's prophecy better than the more popular view that the Antichrist prince—mentioned only in passing in the previous verse—is the sole subject of verse 27 and therefore the one who will make a firm covenant with the Jewish people.

If the partial-fulfillment view is correct, only the second half of Daniel's seventieth week, or three and a half years, remains to unfold at the end of this age. During this relatively short period of time, the events described in the latter portion of verse 27 would be played out on the pages of history. The prophecy states that "on the wings of abominations will come one who makes desolate, even until a complete destruction, one that is decreed, is poured out on the one who makes desolate." This perfectly matches other oracles about the end-time ruler and his ultimate doom.

What does this all really mean? If I and many others are correct in saying that the end-time saints will probably not be caught away before the tumultuous tribulation begins, then those alive at the time may not be facing a seven-year period of worldwide upheaval after all, but one half that length. To sum up, it is better to face a relatively short tribulation period than one twice as long!

THE MAN OF SIN

I will now step out on an olive tree limb (not necessarily recommended) and present a brief, overall scenario that could fit into a shortened end-time framework. Again, this is only a scenario, even if one coming from a journalist and student of prophecy who covers the Middle East every day.

First, the prophesied man of sin will rise to power in some part of the world, probably in Europe, since Daniel links him with the ancient Roman empire. He is called a prince in the prophecies of Daniel, meaning he could well come from regal lineage. His ascension to power may not be automatic, but may involve some warfare, as indicated in Daniel 7:8, where three of the "ten horns" who form his core support group are said to be "pulled out by the roots." This could also imply that the three launch a revolt against him toward the end of his rule

I suspect that the beast's prophesied forty-two-month reign will only officially begin after this process of conquest and consolidation is accomplished. It will probably be preceded or accompanied by global economic and/or social upheaval, along with increasing earthquakes and other natural disasters. Whether the situation is somewhat calm or crisis-ridden, the Antichrist will gain control over the entire earth.

It seems to me that the ten horns, called ten kings in Revelation 17:8, will probably turn out to be ten major world powers. There is no biblical reason to say that they will all be located within the European, North African, and Middle Eastern boundaries of the ancient Roman empire, although the beast's kingdom seems to be centered there.

I suspect that one leg of the man of sin's prophesied world empire will rest on the five major powers of Europe—Germany, France, Spain, Italy, and the United Kingdom. Together, these proud nations contain the bulk of the rising European Union's population base, the lion's share of its economic clout, and most of the continent's military and political muscle. The smaller European Union countries are, quite frankly, window dressing for the emerging superpower. (I apologize for that last comment to my many friends in Holland, Norway, Austria, and elsewhere.) Any one of the smaller countries could be excluded and the federation would still go forward. Nevertheless, they do give the emerging superpower a much greater territorial reach, stretching into the eastern Mediterranean and toward the borders of the former Soviet Union.

I think it is probable that the second leg of the beast's international empire will be comprised of five other non-European world powers. The five would undoubtedly include the United States, which I anticipate will sooner or later play second fiddle to the European Union. America's decline would probably be due to internal economic and racial problems and/or natural disasters, greatly weakening her current colossal strength (a preview of how fast a mighty superpower can implode came with the rapid and generally unforeseen collapse of the expansive Soviet Union, even though the United States is much stronger politically and economically than the USSR ever was). The 2000 presidential election stalemate was just a small reminder of the political, social, and cultural differences and tensions that lie just under the surface in the land of the free and the home of the brave.

The other four foundational nations would surely include China and Russia, but possibly only after European-led wars were fought against the stirring Asian giant and the slumbering Russian bear (this is what I project in my end-time novel). Traditional East-West enmity is still with us despite the demise of the Soviet Union, as was evident during the NATO military assault on Serbia in 1999. That military campaign angered the Russians and Chinese, who saw it as arrogant Western powers imposing their haughty will on a former Communist country. Other pillars in the beast's international empire might be Japan and India, one an economic giant and the other containing one-sixth of the world's population within its borders.

167

The Bible strongly indicates that the Antichrist will somehow become involved in Israel's internal affairs, probably through a revival of the Mideast peace process, which may have previously crumbled in the run-up to a regional war (as we are apparently seeing right now). He would not necessarily "make a covenant" with Israel, as commonly thought, yet still apparently acquire some sort of role as Israel's international protector. There is no biblical evidence that the beast will gain such influence by enacting a final peace treaty between Israel and her neighbors, although nothing in Scripture precludes this. The Antichrist's connection to Israel is inferred in that he will seemingly be interested in a rebuilt temple in Jerusalem—meaning he will obviously need to exert strong political influence in the Lord's land—and in his prophesied command of the final military assault against Israel during the battle of Armageddon.

The treacherous man of perdition will apparently possess supernatural powers, thereby cementing his rule. I suspect the deadly "head wound" that Revelation 13:3 speaks about is an actual fatal injury that is satanically healed. If so, then the Antichrist would be seen to have risen from the dead. My literal approach to this much-debated verse is mainly due to its second half, where it states that "the whole earth was amazed" over this evident healing and therefore "followed after the beast." While this passage may have been difficult to take literally before the age of global satellite communications, it is now entirely possible that people everywhere will view his "resurrection" on videotape, if not on live television. Such a spectacular show would guarantee instant and enormous authority to the "risen" leader.

There has been much speculation (some of it silly) as to who the Antichrist might be. As mentioned above, Daniel calls him a "prince," and I see no reason to discount the insinuation that he will actually come from royal stock. Only time will tell.

I wonder at the propensity of many end-time prophecy addicts to parade the apparent qualifications of this or that potential candidate for all to see. If Revelation 13:3 is literally fulfilled, then it seems probable to me that whoever receives the "fatal head wound" will actually die (what else does fatal mean?), with his body then energized by Satan himself. If this is so, then his predeath political qualifications or international connections may be totally irrelevant. In other words, it may be Satan himself who is the demented genius here, not the slain man whose body he temporarily fills. If so, the devil would be committing the ultimate spiritual fraud by exactly mimicking the Father's full presence in His only begotten Son.

One thing seems irrefutable to me, if not to many others: The Antichrist will *not* be Jewish! The popular notion that he will hail from "one of the tribes" is based on the unbiblical assumption that Israelis will accept him as their long-prophesied Messiah. This is nowhere stated in Scripture.

The man of sin may be highly revered in Israel or even worshiped by many as some illustrious demigod. But there is no evidence whatsoever to suggest that observant Jews—the only ones who nurture substantial messianic expectations—will accept him as their long-awaited Messiah. After all, they are looking for a deliverer who is very much one of their own—who keeps all of the dietary kosher laws, who strictly upholds Jewish religious law, and so on. Indeed, the New Testament suggests that the revered Rabbi from Galilee closely fit that description. But Daniel 2 and 9, supported by the writings of Paul and John, make plain that the evil beast will hardly be a religious Jew. He will come from Gentile background, with his antecedents being four great pagan empires that oppressed the Jewish people in ancient times.

Sadly, the widespread expectation that the Antichrist will be Jewish has added to European anti-Semitism over the centuries. In turn, it has fed Judaism's long-standing reluctance to examine Daniel's end-time prophecies at all, thus leaving Orthodox Jews fairly ignorant of this important sliver of their Bible. This is but one of many sins that the collective church needs to repent of when approaching the Lord's original and enduring covenant people.

I suspect that one of the first projects the satanic world ruler will undertake will be the erection of a magnificent edifice on the Old City's Temple Mount. His spiritual booster, the wonder-working "false prophet" of Revelation 13:11–18, would probably substantially aid him in this endeavor. After the evil pair rule the world for more than three years, they make the mistake of claiming a seat in the phantom Jerusalem temple. There, indicates the apostle Paul, the abominable Antichrist makes his blasphemous claim to be God. Soon afterward the saints of all ages will be translated heavenward to meet their Lord in the clouds, and then God's wrathful vengeance will be poured out on the beast's wicked empire, spelling its imminent demise.

In summary, I believe that the amount of time between the rise of the man of sin to global power and his ultimate destruction will be less than four years. It could take awhile for him to gain complete international control, although I suspect this will be accomplished in a relatively short time span. We are living in an era of unbelievably fast computers and worldwide communication technology, supersonic jets, and lightning-like ballistic missiles. Great battles can be launched and completed in a matter of months, if not weeks, days, or even hours. So even if the beast's ascension to power involves warfare, he could emerge victorious in no time at all.

I believe the Lord's two anointed witnesses will immediately challenge the ruthless world leader. They will be two men that suddenly appear on the international stage, probably in Jerusalem. The three-and-a-half-year ministry they undertake will more or less coincide with the Antichrist's forty-two-month rule. The Lord's prophets will be the visible leaders of the Messiah's worldwide body during the dark days of terror and persecution unleashed by the wicked beast and his lying companion. The abomination of desolation will occur near the end of their public preaching, setting the stage for divine retribution.

The Second Coming will closely follow the slaying of the two prophets in Jerusalem. Although the surviving saints will not know the precise day or hour when their Lord will commence His return, they will recognize the season from events occurring in Israel and the Middle East. On an unknown but glorious day, they will suddenly be caught up to meet their Lord in the air and then return with Him to earth shortly afterward.

Some readers may find my scenario fanciful and amusing. That will certainly be the case with anyone who does not accept the veracity of God's Word. While I obviously could be quite wrong in my apocalyptic interpretations and speculations, I doubt it, since they are based on ancient prophecies delivered by Jewish men who have already proved to be reliable predictors. Claiming to quote the Almighty, these Hebrew seers said the Jewish people would be scattered twice from their land by the Almighty and twice returned. History shows that to be a factual predescription of what has actually taken place. Why should the rest of their prognostications be any less reliable, even if some of my interpretations might be slightly or wholly off the wall?

This end-time overview of what may lie ahead is certainly not comprehensive. Many more prophetic details are contained in Scripture. But I have striven to give an outline that is faithful to the apocalyptic biblical writings. There will surely be surprises—there always are in life. But whatever scenario turns out to be correct, the Lord *will* return in power and great glory, astounding the many skeptical naysayers and thrilling His devoted, longsuffering followers.

10

Earth's Final Battles

===

How do the various wars that are prophesied to take place at the end of the age fit into my end-time scenario? This is another question I frequently field when speaking overseas or to visiting tour groups here in the Promised Land. Such questions became rife when the Palestinians ditched the Oslo peace process and reverted to the path of violence in late September 2000.

Many years of Bible study, combined with intimate knowledge of the land, have led me to conclude that at least two major armed conflicts lie ahead for Israel before the Lord returns to Jerusalem. Having said that, it is possible the various prophecies speak of different aspects of the same war. I believe the saints will still be around for the first battle, the regional conflict described in chapter 5. Indeed, we may see it unfold at any time if recent events are any indication.

However, I think the biblical evidence suggests that the church will be present on earth only during the initial phases of the second war if they witness any portion of it at all. Of course, nobody can be dogmatic about such things, since the predictive Scriptures were patently not designed to give us an exact order of future events, much to many people's chagrin. Stringing bits of antique prophecies together in a workable outline, as I attempted to do when writing *The End of Days*, is not an easy task.

My best guess is that the regional Arab alliance described in Psalm 83 will be formed before the Antichrist comes to power. It will essentially be an attempt by Israel's Muslim neighbors to take back Jerusalem by force. Their "holy war" will end with Israel greatly weakened. Nevertheless, the attacking conspirators will seemingly suffer a devastating defeat, with the renowned Islamic city of Damascus, the second city where Muslim caliphs ruled after Mecca, left in utter ruins. The conspirators' debacle will leave the Arab world ripe for the Antichrist's taking. Most Muslim nations will, however reluctantly, obediently fall into line with his international program. The war will also leave Israel without any threatening enemies along her northern and eastern borders.

The destruction of Damascus will, however, also unleash a worldwide backlash against the tiny Jewish state, as indicated in Isaiah 17:12–13. Many nations will demand that Israel's nuclear weapons be destroyed, as Egypt in particular is already doing. Israel's nonconventional bombs will be replaced by superpower "guarantees" of her future security, probably enacted by the man of sin himself. Significant border defenses and a large standing army will no longer be considered necessary for the country's survival. Although Israeli leaders will surely be more than reluctant to surrender the same, they will do so under intense pressure from their Western allies. The pattern for such a scenario is already evident in the American-sponsored peace process.

An Israel stripped of her major defenses is exactly where Ezekiel's famous "Gog and Magog" prophecy begins. Such a picture is unlikely to develop apart from another regional war in which Israel's neighboring enemies are crushed. Some see Israel abandoning her main defenses solely as a result of the ongoing peace process, but I am certain it will take more than breakable treaties to get any skeptical Israeli government to lay down its powerful swords.

Ezekiel foretold that an alliance of northern-led nations would come up against "a land of unwalled villages" (38:11). This will occur "in the latter years," after the land of Israel is "restored from the sword," and after its inhabitants have been "gathered from many nations to the mountains of Israel which had been a continual waste; but its people were brought out from the nations, and they are living securely, all of them" (v. 8). The prophet says the allied forces will "come like a storm" onto the mountains of Israel, rushing in "like a cloud covering the land" (v. 9).

One can hardly say that modern Israelis have been "living securely" in open villages over the past fifty-plus years. Indeed, fear of enemy attack is always at the back of everybody's mind, given that the nascent Jewish state has been involved in a war every decade until now (1948, 1956, 1967, 1973, 1982, 1991). Indeed, the last major attack, when Saddam Hussein's frightful Scuds came crashing down on heavily populated civilian centers, left Israelis feeling more vulnerable than ever.

Something will seemingly alter the current situation in which Israel is a virtual armed fortress, with very little sense of absolute abiding security. As stated, I suspect the apparent shift to a "peace and safety" mode will result from the Antichrist's irresistible promise to protect diminutive Israel. At the height of his power, he will appear supremely uncontestable, prompting Israelis to embrace his comforting security pact. At any rate, to resist his offer would be impolitic, to say the least.

I anticipate that the prophesied Gog and Magog invasion will be the opening battle in the war that the New Testament associates with the ancient Canaanite town of Meggido, from where we get the famous name Armageddon. All scholars agree that such a battle did not take place in biblical times, although those who view Bible prophecy as mainly symbolic say it could have represented various skirmishes in the ancient world. Certainly the town of Meggido and the surrounding Jezreel valley (where I lived for six months in 1982) have been fought over many times in history. Warfare has been unavoidable given that the strategic area straddles the central coastal plane and Carmel mountain range on one side, the Galilee region on the other, and lies directly north of the disputed hills of Samaria, better known today as the northern West Bank.

Revelation 20:7–8 foretells that an echo of Ezekiel's Gog and Magog invasion will occur at the end of the Messiah's prophesied thousand-year rule. Satan will briefly be released from imprisonment and be allowed to "deceive the nations which are in the four corners of the earth, Gog and Magog, to gather them together for the war." The devil seemingly will be set free in order to test the loyalty of human beings born during the Lord's earthly reign.

Many Christian scholars maintain that the assault described in Revelation 20 will be the only fulfillment of Ezekiel's prophecy. However, the Hebrew seer appears to be outlining an actual invasion into restored Israel

176

that takes place *before* the Messiah King begins to rule from Jerusalem. It seems far more likely that the apostle John has simply borrowed the widely recognized Gog and Magog label and applied it to the prophesied brief rebellion against the Lord at the end of His millennial reign. This does not at all preclude a premillennial, literal fulfillment of the original prophecy.

The military invasion described in Ezekiel 38 is not instigated by Satan, but by a threatening power called "Gog of the land of Magog, the prince of Rosh, Meshech, and Tubal" (v. 2). This power, which lies to the far north (v. 15) of Israel, is not joined by people from around the world, as in Revelation 20, but by certain regional states that are clearly named: Persia, Ethiopia, and Put (v. 5).

Many conservative scholars identify "Gog, prince of Rosh," with Russia, whose capital, Moscow (possibly Meshech in the prophecy), lies just over 1,500 miles due north of Israel. Indeed, there is nothing further north of Israel than the vast country of Russia, apart from the North Pole. In modern terms, Persia clearly refers to Iran. Ancient Ethiopia was located in at least part of the area that the East African country by that name occupies today but also included much of the modern Arab country of Sudan. Put was apparently located due west of Egypt in northern Africa, where Libya lies today.

Israel's powerful God declares that he will intervene to destroy the invading armies by pouring out "a torrential rain, with hailstones, fire, and brimstone" (Ezek. 38:22). Only afterward will the Israeli people acknowledge that their deliverance was accomplished by "the LORD their God," who "made them go into exile among the nations, and then gathered them again to their own land" (39:28). This seems to confirm that Ezekiel's invasion will unfold in the era of the final Jewish ingathering to the Promised Land, long before the war described in Revelation 20. After the wretched invaders are divinely defeated, God proclaims, "I will not hide My face from them any longer, for I shall have poured out My Spirit on the house of Israel" (Ezek 39:29). It is absurd to maintain that God will be hidden from His regathered people during Yeshua's prophesied thousand-year reign in Jerusalem.

Despite its dispirited condition today, I believe that a revitalized Russia will once again make the fatal mistake of launching a military operation against ostensibly vulnerable Israel. Twice before, in 1967 and 1973, the Kremlin sponsored armed assaults on the Jewish state, and each time Russian generals ended up with egg on their face. This time, Moscow will do so in alliance with three of Israel's most notorious regional enemies who are not located directly along her borders, but on the fringes of the Middle East.

It is abundantly evident that the militant Islamic republic of Iran easily fits the enemy bill, with supreme leader Ayatollah Khamenei calling for Israel's complete destruction yet again on December 31, 1999. Putting its money where its mouth is, the radical Muslim country set up and funded the Hizbullah militia that began warring against Israeli forces in southern Lebanon in the mid–1980s. Showing that its war extends to civilians, Hizbullah gunners have occasionally sent rockets across the border into northern Israeli towns and villages. Despite the Israeli army pullout from Lebanon in May 2000, the militia remains a significant force along Israel's northern border.

Sudan is also a militant Muslim country that has been allied with Iran for many years. It has served as a training base for Islamic terrorist groups since the early 1980s. Libya is a rogue country by almost anyone's standards, with strong anti-Israel leanings.

I mentioned in an earlier chapter that many conservative Christian authors and prophecy teachers place the Gog and Magog invasion before the Antichrist comes to power. This is mainly because Ezekiel relates that the rescued Israelis will burn the weapons of their defeated enemies "for seven years" (39:9), which is usually seen to correspond with the expected seven-year tribulation period.

I have no problem with the prospect that the prophesied burning process will stretch into the millennial period, which commences with the Lord's return. On the other hand, I find it highly questionable to propose that the Israelis will experience God's miraculous deliverance before the Antichrist rises to power and then subsequently submit to the beast. Ezekiel makes clear that the Israeli people will know the Lord like never before after the invading armies are crushed, which seems to perfectly fit Zechariah's description of a mass Jewish turning to God at the end of the tribulation period.

It seems to me there is substantial evidence to place the Gog and Magog invasion at the beginning of the final world war, known in Scripture as Armageddon. For one thing, the prophetic description of what occurs to the attacking armies in Ezekiel 39 closely parallels the account of what happens to the Armageddon warriors in Revelation 19. The Lord instructs Ezekiel to command "every kind of bird and . . . beast of the field" to assemble in order to "eat the flesh of mighty men, and drink the blood of the princes of the earth" (vv. 17–18). The military slaughter of those who invade the Lord's land will be so great that the birds and beasts will be "glutted at My table with horses and charioteers, with mighty men and all the men of war" (v. 20). After that, God will set his "glory among the nations; and all the nations will see My judgment which I have executed" (v. 21). They will also then "know that the house of Israel went into exile for their iniquity" (v. 23). Concerning the

Jewish people themselves, God says they will finally "know that I am the LORD their God from that day onward" (v. 22).

The Revelation account of how Armageddon will conclude is virtually identical, although it is a bit grander in scope. An angel cries out to the "birds in midheaven," "Come, assemble for the great supper of God; in order that you may eat the flesh of kings and the flesh of commanders and the flesh of mighty men and the flesh of horses and of those who sit on them and the flesh of all men, both free and slaves, and small and great" (19:17–18). The angelic call to the birds goes forth as the Lord is returning in splendor and glory with His saints (termed "the armies of heaven") to judge the nations and establish His righteous rule (vv. 11–16).

I think it likely that the end of this age will feature a Russian-led invasion of Israel, which will be the first stage of a final world war. The remote northern power will lead a coalition of Islamic states into the Lord's land with the aim of capturing spoil, plundering wealth, and destroying the Jewish people who "live at the center of the world" (Ezek. 38:12). It will not include neighboring Muslim countries that will have been defeated in an earlier war. God Himself will oppose the invaders' insidious action. Their overthrow, I suspect, will occur just prior to the final assault on Israel led by the Antichrist (who could be Ezekiel's Gog, although I doubt it). His invasion will include an incredible two hundred million people from Asia (Rev. 9:16). I expect that the huge eastern army will be largely comprised of Muslims avenging the earlier destruction of Damascus, which might also motivate the prince of Rosh. The Antichrist's forces will suffer the same ignominious defeat as those commanded by Gog, this time at the hand of the visibly returning Messiah.

And Then the End Will Come

All of this is hardly academic to me. Nor is it some funky video game. While I yearn for the return of Israel's Messiah, who laid down His short earthly life as a costly ransom for my sin, I hardly long for the time of trouble that is prophesied to precede His parousia. The Promised Land is no mythical or mystical place to me, as it is to many believers who can only imagine it in their quiet-time musings. It is the land I call home, where I drive my car, pay my rent, buy my groceries, eat my meals, wash my clothes, visit my friends, do my daily work, and go to sleep at night. Its future is very much a part of my daily prayers and concerns.

Although I have substantial faith for Israel's ultimate security and salvation, I nevertheless often fret over the struggle to get there. My anxieties are only calmed and my fears tamed when I open up the Good Book and listen to the awesome, yet soothingly gentle, voice of the Lord.

I often inform my audiences of the time when I broke down and wept while writing my end-time novel. The characters in it were so real to me, especially the believers who were generally composites of actual people I know. The horrendous things I put some of them through were not entirely of my own invention. The scenarios and situations were based on actual prophecies found in the Bible. I firmly expect that, more or less, such stories will unfold one day soon on the pages of history.

"Lord!" I cried out in sorrowful desperation as I was sitting at my computer in southeast Jerusalem working on *The End of Days,* "why are the biblical prophecies so often full of death and destruction? Isn't there any other way You can bring Your promised kingdom to earth?"

181

After weeping into my hands for a few moments, I felt the reassuring voice speaking softly to me. "Son, this earth has a severe case of cancer. It has infected every cell. That cancer is sin. I will operate to remove the diseased tissue. You are writing about that operation, which I have detailed in My Word. It will even involve radiation therapy, as you have written. But do not despair: In the end, the patient will be healed, the cancer will be removed; the earth will be restored and made new."

If I didn't believe what I have just written above, I would hightail it out of the tempestuous Middle East. One does not have to be a tea leaf reader or college professor to ascertain that more nasty troubles lie ahead. This is the region where terrorism began. Dictators like Saddam Hussein, Muammar Kaddafi, and the Iranian mullahs run the show in much of this neighborhood. Chemical and biological weapons abound in this crazy part of the globe, which thrives on ancient hatreds and invidious intrigues. Israel's undeclared nuclear arsenal will soon have its regional twin, if not its triplet. Yes, I'd rush to the nearest exit if I did not believe that I would ultimately see the goodness of the Lord in the land of the living.

Waiting around for Gog, Magog, the Antichrist, and Armageddon is hardly my favorite pastime. Again, I live in a *real* land called Israel with nonvirtual kids playing in actual streets, with smelly cats prancing along massive stone walls, with babies being born in locatable hospitals, with taxi drivers honking their obnoxious horns near apartment building entrances. Reborn Israel—whose restoration was foretold in the sacred Scriptures thousands of years ago—is indeed my home. I love this precious little land and the people living in it, be they individually lovable or not.

If the Russians were to storm across the borders one day while I was still around, I wouldn't shout with glee. I would weep for the dead victims and pray for the injured, even while meditating on the manifest mercy and salvation of our God.

I vividly recall the time when I was working at the Voice of Hope radio station in southern Lebanon, the only gospel media outlet then operating in the entire Middle East. The brutal Lebanese civil war was just beginning to calm down, yet all were wary of sudden flare-ups. In that highly charged atmosphere, I put a scheduled radio program on the reel-to-reel tape recorder one evening in preparation for broadcast. The show, produced in Oklahoma, opened with a familiar jingle.

In his deep southern drawl, the radio evangelist came on to announce that this evening's topic would be Ezekiel 38 and 39. His voice rising with excitement, he described how "the Russian army will swu'eep dauw'un on ta the moun'ains of Israel an ova'run the towns there, killin' people and capturin' spoil all alon' the way! Blood'll flow all over the area! The Israeli people will shu'ly panic, but Gawd has it all under control!"

"The people are probably panicking already!" I proclaimed to myself as I sat listening to the program in the cramped radio studio. Somehow the evangelist's stirring words—delivered with a sort of giddy gusto—didn't sound so exciting from my physical vantage point in the hills of southern Lebanon! I was certain they would strike my northern Israeli listeners in the same peculiar way. I did not condemn the program's host for getting so worked up. After all, Ezekiel's prophecy ends with Israel's miraculous deliverance by her sovereign Lord. But the details are still a bit unnerving, especially if you happen to be living along Gog's probable invasion route.

Yet we who know, serve, and love the Lord can rejoice with copious amounts of joy. Yeshua's word is yes and amen. The Father's plans and purposes for humanity will be accomplished on earth, and nothing will stop them.

The most visible contemporary proof of the veracity of the Bible is the reborn Jewish state, which proclaims God's abiding faithfulness even in Israel's unregenerate condition. As I travel around modern Israel, I cannot help but reflect on Israel's marvelous God, who has also become my Abba Father. By an act of His sovereign will, He joined Himself to His Jewish bride as a husband clings to his wife, just as the Messiah lovingly cleaves to His church. God Himself has become Israel's salvation and mine as well. He is the one who is coming to claim His own. May He come speedily in our day!

Come, behold the works of the LORD,
Who has wrought desolations in the earth.
He makes wars to cease to the end of the earth;
He breaks the bow and cuts the spear in two;
He burns the chariots with fire.
"Cease striving and know that I am God;
I will be exalted among the nations,
I will be exalted in the earth."
The LORD of hosts is with us;
The God of Jacob is our stronghold.

Psalm 46:8–11

David Dolan is an American journalist who has lived and worked in Israel since 1980. He began reporting for CBS Radio News in 1988. He worked before that for CBN News in Jerusalem, for the Moody Radio Network, and for other media outlets. He is a frequent guest on many Christian and secular TV and radio programs and travels extensively around the world.

Dolan's written articles also appear in many publications. He is the author of the highly acclaimed 1991 best-selling book *Holy War for the Promised Land*, which was translated into eight languages and has been updated two times, most recently in 1998 under the title *Israel at the Crossroads*. His second book, also available in various languages, is a fast-moving apocalyptic novel titled *The End of Days*.

The author has written the monthly *Israel News Digest* for the group Christian Friends of Israel since 1986. He also sends out frequent news and analysis updates to thousands of people around the world via e-mail. You may subscribe to the printed *Digest* by writing to CFI, P.O. Box 1813, Jerusalem 91015, Israel. To view his regular Mideast Internet updates, to receive them for free by e-mail, or to purchase his other books, visit his web site at www.ddolan.com.

To schedule David Dolan to speak, phone 800-728-1779 or send a message to: news@cfijerusalem.org